The Integrity of the Church

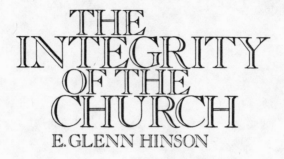

THE INTEGRITY OF THE CHURCH

E. GLENN HINSON

BROADMAN PRESS
NASHVILLE, TENNESSEE

TO
J. D., Jane, Rick, Jay, and Bruce Walton

*who exemplify
the integrity of the church*

Dewey Decimal Classification: 262.7
Subject Heading: CHURCH
Library of Congress Catalog Card Number: 77-82400
Printed in the United States of America

Preface

This is a positive and constructive, even if critical, book. It is written out of the Southern Baptist context but it answers not merely questions which will be found there. Rather, it seeks to wrestle seriously with issues faced by all the churches—indeed, by all humankind. Actually it raises as many questions as it answers, for the important thing now seems to be to ask the right questions, not to find all the answers.

The book represents years of research, reflection, and experience concerning the nature and mission of the church. It incorporates portions of writings that I have published in the past ten years, all fed anew through my mind and heart and, for that reason, essentially new. An important portion has come from *The Church: Design for Survival* (Nashville: Broadman Press, 1967), chiefly chapter 2; a second part from an article entitled "Future Shock and the Christian Mission," *The Quarterly Review* (April—June, 1973), pages 4-16; and a third from an essay entitled "A Theology for the Urban Mission," in *Toward Creative Urban Strategy*, ed. George A. Torney (Waco, Texas: Word Books, Inc., 1970), pages 24-42. Besides these, I have drawn from many other published writings on specific related subjects.

I am indebted to many persons for the insights I have incorporated into the book. If I do not give credit always where credit is due, it is because I have made some thoughts so much a part of myself that I have forgotten where I first latched onto them. In time, I suppose, all of us become what we have experienced. I would express special thanks to colleagues at The Southern Baptist Theological Seminary, who have furnished me with an exciting community of learning; to students, who have constantly picked my brain for better answers than I had; and to my family, who have endured a "spaced-out" father as I have used much of my spare time to put these thoughts on paper.

GLENN HINSON

Louisville, Kentucky

Contents

Part I
Some Preliminary Considerations

1
A New Day for the Church

This is a book about the nature and mission of the church. So much has been written and said on this subject that another book about it might seem superfluous and indefensible. What more can anyone say that will be helpful? Why don't we stop talking about the church and *be* the church for a while?

I am sympathetic with such complaints. Each of us, after all, should be more concerned about being the church and doing what it should do than we are about writing or talking of it. It is not impossible that we will end up like the proverbial lovers who spend so much time planning and plotting every eventuality in their forthcoming marriage that they never get around to marrying. However, there are some questions and arguments to be posed from the other side as well.

One question is: Have we ever grasped and do we ever fully grasp the nature and the mission of the church? Sometimes we become very confident that we have understood them, only to find that they have flitted away like butterflies eluding the collector's net. In the forties and fifties, for example, Christians around the world pronounced confidently with Hendrik Kraemer that "the church is mission." Now they are wondering whether that is so and what that means if it is so. The elusiveness of the nature and the mission of the church points to a second question.

The second question is: Do changing times and circumstances not alter our perception of the nature and the mission of the church? The answer to this question can hardly be anything but a yes. In its history the church has experienced a number of significant shifts in its self-image as times and circumstances have changed. At the outset it adopted a model of the flock from its Palestinian setting.

In its early centuries as an illicit religion in the Roman Empire, it thought of itself as a pilgrim people, a colony of heaven in an alien world. With Constantine's conversion it shifted to the prevailing metaphor of the culture and became the church militant. In the Middle Ages it envisioned itself as the ark of salvation that would bear its passengers to the golden strand, safely piloted by clergy and monks. In early America many Protestant churches took on the town hall motif. Today the churches are influenced more by the business model.

This shifting of images is not in itself a problem. Indeed, it is necessary if Christians want to understand who they are and what they are supposed to do in their own particular eras. Outmoded images, however meaningful in other times and places, will tend to confuse and blur understanding and will not lead to effective action. Some images—for example, the military one during the anti-Vietnam war period—can even create negative feelings and revulsion for what the church is doing. They can thus become counterproductive, even harmful to the churches' work.

Images, therefore, must change with times and circumstances. However, there is a danger that they will shift in such subtle and unnoticed ways that they will not incorporate some of the deeper truths about the nature and the mission of the church. They may even lead the church in the opposite direction from the one it should take. It may become so immersed in current cultural images and paraphernalia, for instance, that it has no identity of its own. It becomes simply a mirror of the culture and not a channel through which God may implement his purpose for humankind.

A reappraisal of the nature and the mission of the church becomes especially crucial in a time of rapid social change such as ours. The church, of course, has confronted the problem of adjustment to change in other eras, but never in the proportions it confronts in the present technological age. The current problem is not just change but, as Alvin Toffler has made clear in *Future Shock*, the accelerated pace of change. In the remainder of this chapter I will summarize Toffler's thesis, delineate some features of the impact that accelerated social change is having on the churches, and look critically at some influential theological proposals for dealing with the problem.

Future Shock

In his widely read book *Future Shock* [1] Toffler tries to demonstrate that "the *rate* of change has implications quite apart from, and sometimes more important than, the *directions* of change" (p. 3). Unless persons are prepared for the rapid *pace* of change, they will fall into a kind of psychological coma that Toffler calls "future shock." To avert this,

> the individual must become infinitely more adaptable and capable than ever before. He must search out totally new ways to anchor himself, for all the old roots—religion, nation, community, family, or profession—are shaking under the hurricane impact of the accelerative thrust (p. 35).

Before we can strengthen our adaptive responses, we must understand what kind of life-style we are now caught up in. The key word is change. Because of the development of technology we have witnessed the demise of permanence. There is no hope of its resurrection either, for technology "feeds on itself"—that is, it produces more technology. Technology is speeding up the pace of life to such an extent that many persons will not be able to cope. It is producing a state of "permanent transience" or "temporariness," novelty, and diversity.

Transience

Transience affects things, places, people, organizations, and information.

With reference to *things,* our age shows its transience in the throwaway paper wedding gown, in the tearing down and rebuilding of buildings, in portable buildings, in modular structures that can be moved from one place to another on short notice, in renting as opposed to buying things, in planned obsolescence, in fad machines, and even in an economics of impermanence.

With reference to *places,* Toffler characterizes us as "the new nomads." Distance has never meant less. Not only are people free to travel almost anywhere; they also migrate freely and change the location of their homes. Geography is dead, and with it has died some of the sense of commitment that went with longer-term relationships.

With reference to *people*, Toffler says, "We have created the disposable person: Modular Man" (p. 97). Instead of becoming involved in the total person, "We plug into a module of his personality" (p. 97). This phenomenon leads to short-term relationships and the formation of different kinds of relationships. It is being reinforced by occupational mobility and by rental of temporary services. Like Harvey Cox, Toffler sees advantages in temporary relationships, a sort of freedom to choose one's friends, but he also notes the stress under which breaking ties places people, especially women. Sometimes this may be traumatic, even when we begin preparing children for it at an early age.

With reference to *organizations*, transience is evidenced in the toppling of bureaucracies—even the Roman Catholic—and in the move toward what Toffler calls "Ad-hocracy." Internal organizational changes occur at a blinding rate. Hierarchies are being replaced by "project" or "task force" management. In the future, organizations will have to possess greater adaptability, consisting of rapidly changing temporary systems. This will mean, in turn, diminished commitments; and commitments will be aimed at tasks rather than at organizations. The organization man will give way to "Associative Man," freed of confining commitments to organization but also placed under strain by having to adapt and relearn.

With reference to *information*, the individual is flooded with a new stock of images that necessitates constant updating in order to be effective. Transience is seen in changing ideas about the education of children, in the short life of books, in the deluge of images produced by the mass media, in symbols we are called on to ingest, in language changes, and in temporary art forms—"the Kleenex tissue of art" (p. 176). Human "image-processing mechanisms . . . are driven to operate at higher and higher speeds" (p. 179). The question is: How much of this will one's neural system take before future shock sets in?

Novelty

Novelty is a second feature of technological society. Novelty is the product of not just an industrial but a superindustrial society. Moving on the line it has been following, our technology is capable of conquering the oceans for human use, controlling the climate, training animals to serve in ways not previously possible, growing microorganisms for human food supplies, creating duplicates of brilliant persons by cloning, replacing all human organs so as to prolong life, and linking up the human brain with computers or conserving the brains of geniuses like Einstein. Many of these possibilities raise serious ethical issues, for they may lead to bizarre and perverse uses, too.

This feature of modern society is leading us from a quest for physical ("gut") satisfaction to one for psychological satisfaction. Technology has induced businesses to become "experience makers." They sell not products but pleasure. Witness, for instance, big airline companies' advertising not just safe, efficient trips, but also "flying the friendly skies."

Increasingly, too, novelty is invading family life. Scientific advances are shattering many orthodox conceptions of the family. Among other things, the superindustrial society's demand for mobility is reducing the size of the family. Changing conceptions of human relationships are opening the way to new types of families and family relationships: professional parents assuming the function of child-rearing for the biological parents, communes, and homosexual fathers and mothers. Transience is also affecting love and marriage, making short-term relationships more and more acceptable, and enhancing demands for freedom.

Diversity

Diversity is manifest in an incredible array of individual choices ("overchoice"), in a surfeit of subcults, and in diversity of life-styles.

Toffler insists that, though technology has produced some types of standardization, radical individualization is more characteristic of it. Superindustrialization is producing "the greatest variety of *unstandardized* goods and services any society has ever seen" (p. 265). Never has there been such a wide range of choice, and we are rapidly racing toward overchoice. Diversity is evident in all sorts of merchandise, in art and education, in movies, radio, and TV. We may be reaching the point where this freedom will become slavery.

In the personal and social sphere modern technological civilization has resulted in heterogeneity. There is an upsurge of subcults in relation to work, recreation, youth, sex and the family, and many other areas.

Finally, superindustrial society, Toffler concludes, "will encourage a crazy-quilt pattern of evanescent life styles" (p. 302). "We are witnessing the crack-up of consensus" (p. 304). Life-style in this age has become a throw-away item.

Toffler sees both dangers and promises in what is happening. The dangers lie in exceeding the limits of human ability to absorb or respond to change. If some attempt is not made to determine the limits, then there may be both a physical and a psychological break-down in future shock. *Physically*, objective studies have shown that the higher the degree of alterations, the more risk there is of illness. Constant confrontation with novelty may exact more wear and tear than the body can stand. Excessive stimulation of human adaptive reaction leads to irreversible deterioration. *Psychologically*, future shock will have about the same effects as combat fatigue. First, evidences of confusion, disorientation, or distortion of reality occur; then signs of fatigue, anxiety, tenseness, or extreme irritability show up; and finally apathy and emotional withdrawal result.

Overstimulation strikes at three levels: (1) the sensory, (2) the cognitive, and (3) the decisional. Individuals vary physiologically in their ability to respond to experiences. But overstimulation interferes *mentally* with the ability to think and to process information. Ultimately it results in an inability to make decisions. Future shocked individuals may react *emotionally* in several ways: by outright denial (that is, blocking out reality); by specialism (narrowing the range of choices); by reversion to previously used adaptive routines which are now outmoded; and by oversimplification. They may react *physically* on parallel lines: by copping out on drugs and artificial trips; by violence; and by withdrawal. Future shock in a large number of individuals may lead to a future-shocked society.

Toffler believes that the solution to these dangers lies not in an avoidance of change but in "a different kind of change" (p. 373). First, the "individual needs new principles for pacing and planning his life along with a dramatically new kind of education" (p. 373). One aspect of this is to periodically take stock of one's physical and psychological reactions to change and subsequently to adjust these reactions. Another is "to control the rates of transience, novelty, and diversity in our milieu" (p. 377). One may do this by building "personal stability zones," which action requires at the same time a radically new orientation toward the future in anticipation of change. However, many persons will not be able to build their own personal stability zones. They will need help. This help may be offered through situational groupings, through crisis counseling, through halfway houses, through enclaves of the past or of the future, and through "global space pageants" which weave into our consciences the "sanity-preserving points of temporal reference" (p. 397).

Adaptability will require an educational revolution, for the present educational methods fitted only the needs of an industrial and not those of a superindustrial society. The goal of the education of the future must be to increase the individual's "copeability" (p. 403); so it must devote more attention to discerning the pattern of the future. The present educational system, therefore, will have to be transformed at three points: in organization, in curriculum, and in orientation to the future. *Organizationally*, there is a need for "dispersal, decentralization, interpenetration with the community, adhocratic administration, a break-up of the rigid system of scheduling and grouping" (p. 409). *In curriculum* nothing should be included that is not going to be relevant for the future, even if this means scrapping much of the present curriculum. Because of the diversity of technological society, the curriculum should offer widely diversified data. However, lest overchoice become a greater problem, it should seek "to create common reference points among people through a unifying system of skills" (p. 413). Students of tomorrow must be taught how to learn and how to choose. In the final analysis, however, education must teach people how to anticipate the future—not of supernatural but of temporal events.

A second response to these dangers is "the conscious regulation of technological advance" (p. 428). We cannot and should not try to stop technology; actually, we need more rather than less of it. The problem is that technology has been allowed to run wild. It has to be brought under control. As the individual makes choices about his or her life-style, so must society make choices about alternative cultural styles. Toffler would ask several questions before allowing technological innovations: (1) What are "the potential physical side effects of any new technology"? (2) What will be "the long-term impact of a technical innovation on the social, cultural and psychological environment"? (3) "Apart from actual changes in the social structure, how will a proposed new technology affect the value system of the society?" (4) What are the "accelerative implications" of each major technological innovation (pp. 437-439)? To assure that these questions were asked, he would set up some machinery for screening—probably a "technology ombudsman."

The third answer to the dangers of future shock is a "strategy of social futurism." Technocratic planning such as we have been accustomed to in the present will not suffice, for (1) it belongs to the fast-vanishing industrial era; (2) it reflects the time bias of industrialism; (3) it was premised on a hierarchy; and (4) it feeds on the philosophy of nowness. What are needed are techniques for measuring transience, novelty, and diversity. That is, planning needs to be humanized. Furthermore, society needs to be infused with "a new socially aware future-consciousness" (p. 459). We must not only predict *probable* but even *possible* futures, which will require not merely a science but also an art. Such planning will necessitate "utopia factories." But the planning must not fall into the hands of state, church, corporations, the army, or the university. It should involve everyone, all of the people, "a continuing plebiscite on the future." Technology has put this within our range.

The Impact of Accelerated Change on the Churches

Future Shock contains many far-reaching implications for our understanding of the nature and the mission of the church. What Toffler has described vis-à-vis contemporary society is obviously affecting and will go on affecting the church itself. It will be helpful to pinpoint some areas in which we may perceive this in relation to the three main characteristics of this age—transience, novelty, and diversity.

Transience

The church, as an institution influenced by its social context, is affected by the transience of *things*. Church buildings rise and fall, like other structures in our society. We hear of portable churches for the beach, forest, or playground during the holiday seasons. Modular structures may become more and more common. Moreover, in view of the cost-use factor, churches are resorting more and more to rental of buildings and equipment.

Transience of *places* has a deeper and more unsettling impact still. The mobility of modern persons means that individual congregations can no longer depend on lifetime service by a sizable number of their constituency. Many churches experience extreme difficulty in getting commitments from their members to do the work of the church and have to rely on the "professionals" to take censuses, witness door to door, teach Bible, and so on. It is not always only a lack of commitment which creates the problem, however; often it is a lack of systematic training to do these things, analogous to children who have received little bits of education under many different systems.

The problem of transience in regard to places is magnified by transience of *persons*. Like other subunits within society, the churches are having trouble developing community. People are fearful of exposing themselves in any significant way to other persons or groups. This preference for anonymity comes out in several ways. Sometimes it means that people will not join a congregation or be involved on more than a casual basis. They opt instead for a private and individualistic kind of religion. At other times it means formal membership without real commitment or involvement. At yet other times it means involvement in a very reserved way. The casually committed person prefers not to risk too much by time-consuming involvement.

Organizational transience is affecting the church just as it is affecting businesses and governments. People are impatient with bureaucracy, as the Roman Catholic Church is discovering in the wake of Vatican II. Among Southern Baptists the agencies have experienced this reaction in terms of suspicion, criticism, hostility, and outright attacks on their programs. To meet the challenge of the times, moreover, these agencies have had to hire consultants to study their structures and advise them concerning new models. They can expect only short-range commitments from employees, also, although the durability is probably conserved somewhat by a long-range Christian commitment.

The churches are being affected by transience in *information*. They cannot feel comfortable any longer in restating old clichés and truisms. They are challenged to adapt language, style, content, and the rest to changing times. They have to seize onto new forms of communication in order to let their symbols penetrate the consciousness of modern man. One example is the TV spot program called *Jot*, which the Radio and Television Commission of the Southern Baptist Convention developed.

Novelty

Novelty as a feature of superindustrial society is having an impact on the religious scene in a number of ways.

1. For one thing, scientific novelties raise many new ethical issues about which the churches have to help give direction. Currently much steam is being generated about abortions, birth-control devices, organ transplants, genetic manipulation, death by decision, and cloning.

2. For another thing, religion is subject to the contemporary stress on what is new and immediately relevant. The past ten years has witnessed a swelling of fads in religion and reactions to them. There are new cults that range all the way from Satanism and witchcraft to hyperfundamentalism.

3. Along similar lines, the experiential element of religion has received special emphasis. The quest for psychological satisfaction is evident in most of the new cults or revivals of old ones. Tongues-speaking is one of the obvious examples.

4. Accompanying the accent on the psychological has been a decline in concern for the rational and institutional aspects of religion. People often have no strong feelings about theology, and certainly none about orthodoxy. They judge one religious system to be as good as another. They have limited appreciation and often strong resentment of programs and institutions. If they gather with others,

they prefer informal settings where they can be open and free.

5. Finally, the church is experiencing the impact of novelity in regard to family life. Families are not as firmly fixed as they once were. Consequently, they tend not to pass on religious outlook and values as they once did. If widespread development of "professional parents" and other new family relationships occurs, we can expect to see even more deterioration of the family as the unit for teaching religion and moral values. Meantime, the single state is becoming more widely accepted as a life-style. Singles include not merely the unmarried or divorced but also single parents who adopt children. Such changes place new demands on the church in trying to conserve some semblance of order at the grass roots of society.

Diversity

Diversity also affects religion.

This fact is immediately evident in *diversity of religious groupings*. America had more than 250 different denominations or cults before the onset of this superindustrial era. Presently we are witnessing the multiplication of subcults everywhere, so that religion takes on the same crazy-quilt pattern we see in society as a whole.

As a result of the multiplication of cults, many people confront the problem of overchoice in religion. Since they are less likely to attach finality to one particular religious form, they hop from one expression of Christian faith to another and from Christianity to other religions. Oriental religions with their occult and mystical character have strong appeal for many college youth. Hinduism, Buddhism, Taoism, Shinto, Islam, and a host of new cults fashioned in imitation of them have been steadily growing in America. Transcendental Meditation (TM) has even wider appeal on account of its pragmatic value in assisting people to cope with life's pressures.

This same trend toward diversity is also affecting the internal makeup of congregations and denominations. Hardly any congregation escapes the tensions of a diverse constituency, which exceed by far those of an earlier and more structured society. The typical congregation, as Ross Mackenzie has observed, in *Trying New Sandals*,[2] is a composite of Baptists, Methodists, Presbyterians, Disciples, Episcopalians, and even Roman Catholics. Moreover, denominational organizations increasingly reflect this potpourri. The Southern Baptist Convention, for example, has always been diverse; but it has grown increasingly so in the past two decades. This helps to account for many of the tensions felt in recent annual meetings.

Growing Individualism

Also involved in the impact of accelerated change on the church is the growth of individual consciousness toward what Charles Reich has called "Consciousness III." Stress on individual autonomy began anew in the Renaissance after centuries during which the church exercised a powerful influence over the individual. It received a new impetus in the Enlightenment of the seventeenth century. In America the frontier enhanced this spirit further. Today we are experiencing a new surge of individualism as a result of the technological revolution.

Consciousness III is affecting the churches in several ways.

First, as in the era of the Renaissance, it is adding to the moral confusion of the times, for it undermines established norms and systems for making moral judgments. Each person does what is right in his or her own eyes, his or her own thing.

Second, it is having a similar impact on thought. The individual decides about his or her own beliefs. He/she does not submit them to peers within the church. If the group tries to dictate, the individual simply drops out. In the United States, for example, the Roman Catholic Church, among others, has witnessed a one-third drop in participation as a result of reaction to Pope Paul VI's refusal to approve the use of contraceptives and the church's stand on divorce.

Third, magnified as it now is, individualism raises some question about how we go about forming congregations and communities, and indeed even whether we should try to form them. Some observers have predicted that the gathered congregation is a thing of the past, others that it will have more limited purposes to serve. Certainly the modular principle will affect the depth and breadth of commitments by individuals to church groups.

The Church Responding to Future Shock

We will return to some of the preceding observations in subsequent chapters when we look at some ways in which the churches may respond to rapidly accelerated social change. Before the conclusion of this chapter, however, a brief general word should be said about alternative Christian responses to accelerated change.

Instinctively, some individuals and groups will respond as Toffler has predicted in *Future Shock*. They will deny the need for change, opt for a few things in which they feel comfortable, revert to told routines, or oversimplify the problems at hand. They will cop out, become belligerent, or withdraw. B. F. Skinner's proposal that our society exercise rigid control over the behavior of its citizens perhaps represents the extreme form that the conservative reaction to change may take.

Others will respond with a rubber stamp. They will approve any and all changes, happy only if nothing remains of the old and tradition-worn. They will seek and cultivate fads. That, at any rate, was the direction taken by many Roman Catholics when the Second Vatican Council opened the windows and doors for *aggiornamento* or "updating" of the Church.

However sympathetic one may be to both of these groups, I would argue, as I did in *The Church: Design for Survival*, that the church should follow neither of these courses. It should not change merely for the sake of changing, but neither should it lock itself into outmoded patterns of the past. *At one and the same time it should strive to conserve its identity while engaging in its mission in and to the world with adaptability or flexibility.* This can be done if we will keep as our point of reference who we are and what we are to do as the church—namely, if we will keep in mind the nature and the mission of the church.

Christianity seems particularly well suited to meet the challenge of rapid social change. In its better moments it has always maintained an openness to the future in the conviction that we "do not have an enduring city here" but that God is directing what is only a mixed and incomplete version of his purpose toward some ultimate goal. The adjustment that we are now having to make is in part a return to root principles. The *new* and shocking aspect of the present era is the *magnitude* of change we are summoned to face; it is not the change itself.

2
An Approach to a Problem

The preceding chapter stated that coping with change will necessitate an understanding of the nature and mission of the church in terms of present times and circumstances. All who have wrestled with this challenge will recognize that such understanding does not emerge automatically. Like personal self-understanding, understanding of the nature and mission of the church requires an extensive inventory of the complex factors that help to explain what the church is and what it is to do. To be precise, it requires an awareness of the church's origins, its history, and its present social matrix.

This study of the nature and mission of the church will reflect a measure of insight from each of these areas. The axle around which the study will revolve, however, will be what is disclosed of the nature and mission of the church in the Old and New Testaments. To locate the center here is not to deny or denigrate the importance either of the centuries-long experience of the church or of its present experience. Both historical and sociological studies are needed to shed much light on the subject.

However, I have chosen to let the light of history and present experience illuminate what can be gleaned from the Scriptures concerning the nature and mission of the church for several reasons: (1) I presuppose that the Scriptures contain the revelation of God concerning the nature and purpose of humanity in general and of the church in particular. (2) More specifically, I am convinced that this revelation is bound up and particularized in Jesus of Nazareth, fulfiller of Israel's hopes under the old covenant, and that what can be known about this revelation in Jesus is to be found almost exclusively in the New Testament. (3) I judge that the experience of the first Christians as the church has a normative character that sub-

sequent experience cannot have. Their experience is normative because it was tied up with a never-to-be-repeated experience of Jesus'
life, death, and resurrection. To be sure, the risen Christ is still present
in and through his church, but not in the same way he appeared
to those first witnesses. Observe, at any rate, Paul's admission that
his experience of the risen Christ was out of the ordinary. Christ
appeared, he said, to Cephas, then to the twelve, then "to more than
five hundred brethren at one time," then to James, then to all the
apostles. "Last of all, *as to one untimely born,* he appeared also
to me" (1 Cor. 15:4-8). Paul did not expect a repeat performance.
(4) Finally, I believe that, in reporting on the life of the church
through several centuries under the old covenant and nearly one
century under the new, the Scriptures manifest evidences both of
what, by divine intention, the church ought to be and of what, by
human experience, it actually is and has been.

It is in the latter area, of course, that Christianity's experience
in history and in the present add color to the portrait. But we cannot
be content merely to describe what is and has been. We need also
a blueprint or a model by which we can evaluate how well the
actuality suits the divine intention.

Focusing the study in this way would seem to simplify the task
a great deal and to assure a measure of consensus among all Christians.
Unfortunately, although it may achieve both of these objectives to
some degree, the perenially vexing issue of interpreting the Scriptures
stares us in the face. How are we to discern what the Scriptures
say concerning the nature and mission of the church? A brief glance
at the history of writings about the nature and mission of the church
readily confirms that consensus is not possible unless and until Christians agree on a common method of interpretation.

A Disputed Doctrine

Until recent years, most statements on the nature of the church
have been composed with a polemical intent by divided Christians.
Each church or sect has written to defend its own reason for existence
and to attack similar claims by its opponents or competitors. In
the early centuries, for example, the Donatists of North Africa
claimed to be the only church that met the biblical standard of

purity and thus refused to recognize baptisms, ordinations, or other observances of Catholics. Catholics replied by insisting that the Scriptures do not presuppose a pure church in the sense of purity of each of its members but a mixed body of saints and sinners (wheat and tares). They then proceeded to disenfranchise the Donatists by saying that, because of their divisiveness, they lost an essential qualification for being the church—namely, love.

In the Middle Ages also numerous sects defined the church in such a way that they could validate their separateness and invalidate that of the church of Rome, from which they had withdrawn. Some sects, for example, those calling themselves the *Cathari* ("pure"), emphasized purity as the Donatists had. Others, such as the Arnoldists, evidently stressed poverty and identification with the masses. Still others, notably the Waldensians, put literal adherence to certain teachings of Jesus and evangelical preaching at the center. Judged by these criteria, the Roman Church had lapsed, and the sects appeared as the true church. Rome, of course, replied by citing the well-known text about Petrine primacy and the keys of the kingdom (Matt. 16:18). The fact that it had recourse to secular powers which the others did not have assured that, in the long run, Rome would win.

The Protestant Reformation heightened further the tendency to define the nature and mission of the church along defensive and polemical lines. Luther and Calvin, for example, exploited the dichotomous concept of the church—that is, visible and invisible, developed in the fourteenth century by John Wyclif. Such a concept was based much less on the Scriptures than on a concern to explain the divisions that had already developed. Wyclif, of course, framed his view in the context of the papal schism of 1378. To explain how one person could *claim* to be the pope and still not be the pope, he applied the theory of a visible and invisible church. The invisible church consists only of the elect. A pope, though head of the visible church, may not be a member of the invisible church—one of the elect. Consequently, he may make a false claim.

Luther and Calvin applied this same theory to the divisions within Christendom as a result of their reform movements. They made a strong point of the fact that, whatever control Rome might claim to exercise over the church visible, it could not do the same for the church invisible. God alone could exercise that prerogative. At the same time all of the reformers insisted that they could assure apostolicity and thus validity for their movements by returning to the apostolic pattern for the church found in the New Testament. Both Luther and Calvin contended that the church is to be seen where the Word of God is rightly preached and the sacraments properly administered. Both, but Calvin more than Luther, strove to develop institutional patterns that they thought Scriptures modeled. The Anabaptists proceeded even more radically to try to implement the biblical pattern of the gathered church, making much of personal regeneration and discipline and striving visibly to obtain the pure church.

Rome responded in a predictable way by reasserting its claims to primacy and authority based on the succession of bishops from Peter. The Council of Trent further widened the breach between Catholics and Protestants, however, by claiming two sources of authority—Scriptures and tradition. This action meant in effect that the Church in the person of the pope as final interpreter of both would have the final say in all things. Even more than the decrees of the Council of Trent itself, the Profession of the Tridentine Faith to which Catholics were required to subscribe revealed what a fait accompli the hierarchical, institutional church had achieved. The convert to Catholicism was required to hold the sense of Scriptures taught by "our holy mother Church," to "acknowledge the holy Catholic Apostolic Roman Church for the mother and mistress of all churches," and to "promise and swear true obedience to the Bishop of Rome, successor to St. Peter, Prince of the Apostles, and Vicar of Jesus Christ." [1]

For nearly four centuries after this the lines between Protestant and Catholic hardened as each side defended itself as the true representative of Christianity and excoriated the other as an apostate. The defensiveness perhaps reached its peak in the nineteenth century as various denominations became increasingly sensitive about their legitimacy. Growth of religious indifference and even hostility to religion figured prominently in this, of course. Both Catholics and Protestants feared the accompanying latitudinarianism (the view that one expression of Christianity is as good as another). Many in both groups, therefore, responded with claims of finality for their own denomination.

On the Protestant side this exclusive claim came to expression among Baptists, to cite one instance, in the phenomenon known as Landmarkism. Arising in the mid-nineteenth century in Tennessee, Landmarkism claimed in effect to represent the *only* true church. Against Catholic claims of apostolic succession through bishops, it offered a theory of Baptist church succession by way of the sects of early and medieval Christianity. There were always Baptist churches, it was argued. Sometimes they were not visible, but they existed nevertheless. They became clearly visible in the seventeenth century. These churches exhibited the true marks ("Landmarks") of Christianity: (1) The local church is the only true expression of the church, the kingdom of God on earth. (2) The only true churches are those that practice believers' baptism. Those which practice infant baptism are not gospel churches. (3) Baptisms can be recognized as valid only if performed in Baptist churches. (4) Communion may not be shared with any person who has not received Baptist baptism. (5) None except Baptist ministers should speak from the pulpits of Baptist churches, because non-Baptist ministers are not gospel ministers.

Contemporaneously the Roman Catholic Church reacted defensively to a variety of threats to its claims of finality by intensifying those claims. In 1864 Pope Pius IX soundly condemned latitudinarism and indifferentism, including the view that "Protestantism is nothing more than another form of the same true Christian religion, in which it is possible to be equally pleasing to God as in the Catholic Church." [2] In 1870 the First Vatican Council secured papal authority by making papal infallibility a dogma. While it is true that the decrees of this Council in effect limited claims some would make for the infallibility of the pope, it also drove in further a nail that Trent had left partially protruding.

The Council declared that "by the appointment of our Lord (see Matt. 16:18) the Roman Church possesses a superiority of ordinary power over all other churches," so that all Christians everywhere owe the bishop of that church "hierarchical subordination and true obedience." This position is assured by the "dogma divinely revealed" that the pope, "when he speaks *ex cathedra*, that is, when in discharge of the office of pastor and doctor of all Christians, by virtue of his supreme Apostolic authority, he defines a doctrine regarding faith or morals to be held by the universal Church, by the divine assistance promised to him in blessed Peter, is possessed of that infallibility with which the divine Redeemer willed that his Church should be endowed for defining doctrine regarding faith or morals; and that therefore such definitions of the Roman Pontiff are irreformable of themselves, and not from the consent of the Church." [3]

The Protestant lines of defense began to topple in the early twentieth century as concern for the world mission of Christianity gave encouragement to united effort. By 1954, when the World Council of Churches held its second assembly, at Evanston, Illinois, Protestants were beginning to be able to look more sympathetically at one another's doctrines, including their understanding of the nature and mission of the church. At the same time they discovered also that they could study the Bible together and, applying modern historical methods, come out with similar conclusions, sometimes supportive and sometimes not supportive of their own claims.

Roman Catholics slackened their defenses more slowly. Pope John XXIII (1958-1963), hoping for a new Pentecost, opened the way for this. He began calling Protestants "separated brothers" and referred to Protestant denominations as "churches." Then the Second Vatican Council, which John himself inaugurated but which he did not live to see completed, redefined the nature and mission of the church along scriptural lines. Although the Council retained some of the institutionalist perspective developed over several centuries and reaffirmed the dogma of papal infallibility, it also recovered for Roman Catholics the biblical imagery of the people of God and the pilgrim people. More significant still, it laid aside the two-source theory of authority of the Council of Trent and opted for a one-source theory. The one source is, of course, divine revelation, the Word of God.

A debate now rages over the extent to which all tradition in the church must be checked by revelation found in the Scriptures. It is very clear, nevertheless, that with this decision Catholics and

Protestants have drawn nearer to one another in their ability to understand the nature and mission of the church than they have been since the early sixteenth century.

Searching the Scriptures

Ironically, while Catholics and Protestants have been drawing closer together, another division between Christians has widened. This division is not a Catholic-Protestant one. Rather it divides most denominations. Although Catholics and Protestants are debating the issue from slightly different angles, the split focuses on the matter of using historical methodology to interpret Scriptures and tradition and in the formulation of doctrine. This issue is sufficiently crucial to a proper definition of the nature and mission of the church that I must explain my own position within the larger context of debate.

The Debate in Roman Catholicism

Within the Roman Catholic Church the controversy has centered around the dogma of papal (and church) infallibility decreed by Vatican I and reaffirmed by Vatican II. The brilliant young Tübingen theologian Hans Küng [4] has argued that this doctrine was historically conditioned, a product of fears of liberalism and nineteenth-century political struggles in Europe, and should be abandoned. Indeed, he goes on to say that no proposition can be declared infallible. God alone can be called infallible. All things human are fallible. The church is fallible. History confirms that popes and councils can err and have erred. It would be better, then, from the standpoint of modern concern for truthfulness, for the church to admit that it can and does err. The church should claim no more than to be faithful to the truth "despite error." How, then, is the church to arrive at certainty?

Küng has proceeded to argue that, according to the one-source theory of the Second Vatican Council, all dogmas must be answerable to the divine revelation contained in the Scriptures. Scriptures are the norm by which all doctrines should be tested. While some dogmas may have a normative place in the life of the church, all must be squared with the Scriptures. Dogmas are "normed norms," Scriptures alone an "unnormed norm." Not even they can be called infallible, however, Küng insists. They too reflect the human. They occupy an ultimately normative place by virtue of being at the headstream of revelation, but they are not revelation itself.

In the final analysis, according to Küng, Catholics, Protestants, and Orthodox all need to surrender claims to infallibilty. Catholicism needs to give up the claim to church and papal infallibility, Protestantism to infallibility of the Bible, and Orthodoxy to the infallibility of the first seven ecumenical councils.

Considering the traditional stance of Roman Catholicism regarding dogma, it is not surprising that even so eminent and respected a theologian as Karl Rahner expressed some surprise at Küng's view and quickly labeled him a "liberal Protestant" and possibly a "skeptic." Protestant—because Küng placed the authority of the Scriptures above all dogmas and refused to accept any dogma as per se normative. Liberal—because he denied infallibility even to the Bible. Skeptic—because he questioned the possibility of formulating propositions that could be considered absolutely reliable. The question that is posed ultimately is: How far does one go in doubting the church's teachings? Even if the church is human, does the Holy Spirit not preserve its efforts to formulate dogmas in such a way that some propositions are not subject to error? Or are all propositions unreliable, thus leaving no ground of certainty?

The Debate in Protestantism

Within Protestantism the controversy has focused on the infallibility and/or inerrancy of the Scriptures. This debate is not new. Rather, it goes back to the nineteenth-century application of the methods of historical criticism to the Bible, first in Germany and then elsewhere in the West. It has heated up again recently, however, as the use of critical-historical methodologies has crept into conservative or evangelical ranks. Concurrently, the study of religion on the periphery of the church—for example, in state universities—has led to increasingly radical results.

The alarm of conservative evangelicals is understandable. They can call history to witness for the fact that abandonment of biblical inerrancy has sometimes been followed by abandonment of belief in other biblical teachings, including critical articles of faith, and eventually, to use Harold Lindsell's word, "apostasy." It is quite possible and frequently happens that scholars become so imbued with the application of critical methods of the Scriptures that they treat them just like any other variegated collection of literature and overlook altogether their religious message. They discount all claims of inspiration save for that shared by human literature in general. To them the object is to understand what the fully human authors said and what social or cultural factors shaped their thinking. As the scientific study of religion becomes more and more a subject for universities, which explicitly deny affiliation with the churches, the danger is real enough. Moreover, the university orientation may easily carry over into colleges and seminaries that do serve the churches.

In reacting to the danger from this extreme, however, conservative evangelicals have gone too far in the opposite direction in repudiating the use of the historical critical method to interpret the Scriptures. The net effect of this rejection is to create a credibility problem for persons whose thought patterns have been shaped by modern scientific methodologies and criteria. The problem, as Hans Küng has pointed out, is precisely one of truthfulness; and no piling up of assertions not backed up by believable data and arguments will get around this demand. Many persons will accept statements about the Bible, as about other things, on the basis of logical, empirical evidence.

According to Harold Lindsell in *The Battle for the Bible*, evangelical Christians must insist upon the infallibility and inerrancy of the Scriptures in the original autographs, which we admittedly do not and never will have, in all facets of information they supply—scientific, historical, religious. "The Bible is not a textbook on chemistry, astronomy, philosophy, or medicine," he conceded. "But when it speaks on matters having to do with these or any other subjects, the Bible does not lie to us. It does not contain error of any kind." [5] Lindsell does not want to support inerrancy by means of a mechanical or "dictation" theory of inspiration. Those who wrote the books of the Bible were human beings. However, he insists that the Holy Spirit so inspired the human authors that no error could intrude. Supposed errors and contradictions can all be explained by slips that occurred in the process of transmission of the text.

The Bible, therefore, is to be interpreted and believed as it stands. If an interpreter begins to apply the canons of modern historical criticism, he or she will discount the work of the Spirit in inspiration and undermine the authority of the Bible. The long-range effects will be disastrous. "It will result in the loss of missionary outreach; it will lull congregations to sleep and undermine their belief in the full-orbed truth of the Bible; it will produce spiritual sloth and decay; and it will finally lead to apostasy." [6]

Another Perspective on Historical Study of the Bible

Sympathetic as I am with those who believe the Scriptures should play a normative role in the formulation of Christian doctrine, I would point to several flaws in Lindsell's thesis.

First, it is questionable whether the Bible itself supports a theory of infallibility and inerrancy such as Lindsell argues for. Certainly neither of these words has been applied to Scriptures in the New Testament. Moreover, the texts he cites (2 Tim. 3:16-17; 2 Pet. 1:21; 1 Thess. 2:13; 1 Cor. 14:37; Gal. 1:11-12) simply claim *inspiration* and in no way sustain the idea of infallible and inerrant inspiration of every syllable, original autograph or not. On the contrary, one may cite clear evidence—for example, in Paul's directions for the unmarried and widows in 1 Corinthians 7—that the writers of Scripture did not claim *absolute* inspiration! Observe in 1 Corinthians 7:10 and 12 how Paul differentiated *his* word from the word of the Lord. While the word of the Lord was command, his word was advice. This is extremely instructive because it obviously followed in the train of Jesus' claims of authority vis-à-vis the Old Testament. Jesus' own authority stood above not merely *interpretations* of the Jewish Scriptures of his day but of the Scriptures themselves. *He* could correct Moses—that is, the Pentateuch (Matt. 5:21 ff.; 19:7-8). The apostle Paul unquestionably believed that Jesus' word stood above his own.

Secondly, Lindsell's major argument is purely pragmatic, by his own admission intended to be alarmist. It runs: If we do not consider the Bible infallible and inerrant in all its parts, then we will start surrendering the truths it teaches one by one until we have apostatized from the faith altogether. His favorite witnesses (should I say "whipping boys"?) are the Unitarian Universalist Association and Union Theological Seminary in New York. Even if these two examples stand, and that is doubtful, I would ask: Does it necessarily follow that laying aside the concept of inerrancy will *always* lead to the other? More thorough study of the history of the church will not sustain the supposition.

Actually, a historian can make a better case for an inverse hypothesis. If we consider the Bible infallible and inerrant in all its parts, as Christians did during the Middle Ages and Reformation, we will apostatize from what it teaches by letting bigotry create an excess of zeal to make everyone believe what we believe. One thing the onset of the age of critical studies has done is to help us avert inhumanity to others. More important still, critically informed Christians in our day may come closer to implementation of the Bible's teachings about equality of the races and sexes than their forebears who believed the Bible infallible and inerrant.

Thirdly, while it is to be conceded that Christians consistently held to the theory of an infallible and inerrant Bible until the nineteenth century, it is important to make some qualifying observations about *omissions* in Lindsell's argument. One has to do with the canon of Scriptures. Which books belong to the Bible has never been fully answered. Luther, one of Lindsell's chief witnesses for infallibility and inerrancy, highhandedly departed from the Old Testament canon used in the church until his day and dismissed James as "a right strawy epistle." Moreover, early Christianity did not settle on a New Testament canon until near the end of the fourth century and then did not achieve universal agreement. Today some Christian canons of the New Testament have twenty-two, some thirty-five, and some twenty-seven books! Which of these are in toto inspired?

A second observation concerns the origins of the theory of inspiration, which dominated for many centuries. Most scholars are of the opinion that it derived from the Greek theory of inspiration of mantic prophetesses (for example, the Delphic oracle). This theory, which appeared first in the early Christian apologists of the second century and not in the New Testament, leaned toward a more mechanical concept of direct inspiration than the Jewish concept of God delivering his word through prophets by illumination of their perception regarding certain events.

A third observation involves the development of historical methodology. Through many centuries the church has used methods of interpretation current at the time. In the first several centuries there were two methods, not one. One, drawn out of the Jewish matrix, *approached the Scriptures historically*. It found its best representation in the "school" of Antioch in the fourth century, whose view of inspiration by no means coincided with Lindsell's "every jot and tittle" view. The other, borrowed from Stoic methods of interpreting Homer, *interpreted the Scriptures allegorically*. It suited well the concept of plenary verbal inspiration, for it did not have to pay much attention to historical accuracy. Since Christianity eventually consisted largely of converts from Greek and Roman culture, the second method dominated. In the nineteenth century, however, there was a recovery of historical methodology in the West. It was natural that this should again be applied to interpretation of the Scriptures. The fact that the method has sometimes been subjected to abuse should not cause us to abandon it.

Fourthly, Lindsell's efforts to explain discrepancies of a historical or scientific nature in the Scriptures appear highly contrived. They steer around problems rather than solve them. The problems are far more serious than he allows. Such an approach will not satisfy persons concerned for letting evidence speak for itself, as Lindsell wishes us to achieve for the Bible.

A Still Better Way

To turn to the positive side of the issue, the purpose of using the methods of the historian in interpreting the Scriptures is to understand as well as we can their religious message. The writings of the Old and New Testament are historical documents. In them, we believe, "In many and various ways God spoke of old to our fathers by the prophets; but in these last days he has spoken to us by a Son" (Heb. 1:1-2). The best way to get the message, the word of God, is by letting historical disciplines help us. These methods will help us find the most reliable text. They will help us construct the times and context in which the Scriptures were written. They will help us become acquainted with the authors. They will help us interpret the meanings of words, sentences, paragraphs, and whole writings.

What we must recognize, as even Lindsell admits, is that Scriptures are not single-tiered. They are not like a one-layer cake. Just as the author of Hebrews recognized, we too must recognize that God spoke to men of old "in *many* and *various* ways." There is, to be sure, a consistent message that ties all of the Scriptures together. It has to do with the loving God's efforts to bring all humanity into fellowship with himself through his people. But this theme comes out in various times and places and circumstances in highly diversified modulations. Only searching study, the application of the best historical methods available, will enable us truly to grasp the word of God within the Scriptures.

To consider this matter specifically with reference to our study of the nature and mission of the church, we can say, on the one hand, that both Old and New Testaments tell the story of the people of God. The Old Testament recounts the story of the people under the old covenant. The New Testament recounts it under the new covenant. In this very distinction, however, we can see that the Old Testament will not have the same authority as the New in shaping our understanding of the nature and mission of the church. What Israel under the old covenant perceived as God's purpose was reinterpreted by Israel under the new covenant. Consequently, when we look for a final word, we look to the New Testament, as Christians always have.

But the New Testament itself is not single-tiered either. It contains the words of Jesus, which for Christians have had a normative significance no other words could have. That is so because we believe God's revelation reached some kind of final expression in him. In him, as John put it, "the Word became flesh and dwelt among us" (John 1:14). Ultimately it is to him, then, that we look for a proper understanding of God's purpose for his people. Once again, however, it is not superfluous to point out that apart from exacting historical research we cannot discern what Jesus intended of the church. The Gospels, which contain almost all that we know about him, do not contain a discourse by Jesus on the topic. Indeed, Jesus' sayings in the Gospels allude to the word "church" (*ekklesia*) only twice, both times in Matthew. Hence, it is the task of historical research to ferret out his intention for the church in other ways.

Considered as a whole, the writings found in the New Testament recount the earliest Christians' experience of Christ and the church, covering roughly a century. There is a common theme for the experience, related to the conviction that "God has made him both Lord and Christ, this Jesus whom you crucified" (Acts 2:36). It can scarcely be questioned that it was the conviction that God had raised Jesus from the dead, thus fulfilling Old Testament promises. This conviction brought the church into existence, gathering a badly disillusioned band of followers into an army of witnesses. The sine qua non for the church was a confession of Jesus' lordship based on belief in his resurrection (Rom. 10:9).

However, the writings of the New Testament reflect also the kaleidoscopic ways in which the early converts grasped this central truth and expressed it. Human beings laid hold on Jesus and his message and applied it in a variety of ways. To be sure, there is one gospel. Paul left no doubt about that fact (Gal. 1:7). But that one gospel is transmitted through several evangelists, each adding his own touch. It was in recognition of both the oneness and the variety of expression that early Christianity entitled our Gospels as it did: *The* Gospel . . . according to Matthew, . . . according to Mark, . . . according to Luke, . . . according to John. We could add: . . . according to Paul, . . . according to Peter. It does not require more than casual reading to see that John packaged the gospel in a different wrap than Matthew, Mark, and Luke. Increasingly, through historical study, we see that Matthew, Mark, and Luke also had distinctive wraps, despite their dependence on one another.

These early Christians also used different forms to express their faith as communities. This is illustrated by the diversity of their styles of worship. In Jerusalem the first Christians continued to worship in the Temple for a time. Elsewhere, both in Palestine and outside it (Acts 9:20; 13:5,14; 14:1; 15:21), they went to the synagogues until forced out. But they also met in specifically Christian settings to share a fellowship meal and to observe the distinctively Christian meal that we call the Lord's Supper (Acts 2:42; 1 Cor.

11:17-34). At other times they held prophetic services (1 Cor. 14). The same variety in forms is illustrated also by a diversity of church polities.

It is no longer possible, if it ever was, to defend the view that the New Testament sustains only one church polity—episcopal, presbyterian, or congregational. The truth is, one may find evidence of all three among the diverse communities of the first century. The Jerusalem community exhibited something like an episcopal structure headed by James, Jesus' brother, and the twelve. Several writings give evidence of communities with a presbyterian type of structure (1 Tim. 3; 4:14; Titus 1:5 ff.). Corinth evidently had a congregational one (2 Cor. 2:6).

Of course, some persons will find an emphasis upon unity and variety of early Christian experience bewildering and perhaps disturbing. All of us are more comfortable with unambiguous facts or solutions to problems. As unsettling as the discovery may be, however, it may help us to see more clearly the twofold challenge which lies before us in studying the nature and mission of the church. On the one hand, we are interested in discovering the *essence* of the church's nature and mission, insofar as we can determine that. Even here, of course, it is possible that we will not be able to obtain a single answer in searching the Scriptures. We must recognize that even in those places where we are most likely to discern the essence, in images or figures applied to the church in the New Testament, we will see great variety. Paul Minear has discussed nearly a hundred such images without exhausting all of the possibilities. Nevertheless, closely examined, most of the images, especially the most important ones, are interconnected and give us insight into the essential nature and mission of the church.

On the other hand, we are also interested in how to be the church and how to do what it is supposed to do *in our own age*. Here the diversity of early Christian experience in being the church may be more instructive than disturbing. First of all, it reminds us that we do not need to feel tied down to certain conventions and stereotypes, even those of the first century. Rather, we are free to develop programs and institutions that will achieve the purposes of the church. This does not mean, of course, that we will disregard the past and experiment in a willy-nilly fashion. Certain forms, such as baptism and Lord's Supper, were almost universally observed in early Christian churches, expressing as they did aspects of the very essence of the church. How these forms were incorporated into worship rites, however, was another matter. The churches did not feel slavishly bound to fixed forms—at least not until the time of Constantine, when uniformity served as a political purpose.

Secondly, the variety encourages us to respond sensitively to the social and cultural situation of the church in our own age. The New Testament already reflects clearly two vastly different cultural milieu—Jewish and Hellenistic. Hellenists like Stephen and then the apostle Paul dislodged Christianity from a cultural fixation in Judaism. To be a universal faith Christianity had to obtain this freedom. In Paul's words, "I have become all things to all men, that I might by all means save some" (1 Cor. 9:22). In opting for such an approach, however, we must be careful that we do not lose our bearings, swallowed up by our culture to become a culture religion. Early Christianity's experience shows us the danger here, but it also confirms the necessity of risking adaptation.

Thirdly, the variety teaches us not to be discouraged because we find it difficult to be the church and to fulfill its mission. We share this difficulty with early Christianity. Those first Christians were obviously uncertain about Jesus' intention. Some thought he wanted to restrict the mission of the church to Israel, others that he envisioned a world mission. Some held on tightly to the customs of Judaism such as circumcision; others let them go in order to win Gentiles. They did not have patented answers to problems that confronted them. They struggled even as we struggle to be the church.

Part II
The Nature of
the Church

importance
of images

3
Images of the Church

collective

Human beings incorporate their deepest experiences in images they carry around in their minds and use to communicate with others about them. "One picture is worth a thousand words," we often say. But behind every word we employ lies some kind of image imprinted upon our brains. Otherwise, words would mean nothing. A child learns first from pictures, then from words.

Some images have much greater significance for us than others. Just hearing a word that stands for a certain image may trigger the remembrance of a whole chain of experiences. The word *mother*, for example, arouses instantly in my mind memories of soft hands caressing my hair, the gentle swaying of a rocking chair, covers being gently tucked under my chin against the chill of winter's night, severe scolding about chores left undone, the sting of a peach tree limb across bare legs for "sassing," and many other images space will not allow me to record.

As pregnant as some images are with meanings, none will suffice to describe in full what we want to say. Neither a word nor an image can communicate the totality of an experience—for instance, an experience of the church. That is why the first Christians used many word pictures when they spoke about the church. That is also why it is necessary for us to consider several of the more frequently used images that they used, in this case four. We must understand, of course, that these four images do not exhaustively describe an experience that means to us what the church has meant through the centuries. They convey at best some key facets of this experience.

The image of the new humanity is perhaps the broadest image in its implications. It depicts the church from the point of view of the divine purpose in creation and redemption—God's creation and re-creation of humankind to share fellowship with himself. The image of the people of God links the church to God's selection of Israel from among all nations to be his people and to engage in the task of reconciling humanity to himself. The image of the servant represents the early church's and perhaps Jesus' own understanding of the means of which Israel would discharge the divine mission—that is, by pouring out its life in service rather than by conquest of terrestrial enemies. Finally, the image of the city of God points up early Christianity's understanding of its temporary status in the world. Each of these images, as well as others that will be mentioned incidentally, is ripe with implications concerning the nature and the mission of the church.

The New Humanity: the Body of Christ

The concept of the new humanity or the body of Christ, developed especially by Paul, is rooted in the Jewish-Christian understanding of the creation and fall of humanity. Hence, before looking at its implications for the church, we must deal briefly with these two ideas.

The question that immediately confronts us here is "Why the creation?" From his own point of view, God created humanity because it is his nature to create. Paradoxically, he did not have to create and yet he did have to. His own nature, which one early Christian called *agape* love (1 John 4:8), compelled him to share his own life, somewhat as a mother's love compels her to bear children.

From the human point of view, on the other hand, God created human beings to share his life and what he had made. Though foreseeing anguish and suffering for both human beings and himself, he foresaw also the value of fellowship between his creature and himself.

This divine-human fellowship depended, of course, on voluntary response. Consequently, God created human beings free, able to respond in love to his love. Like God himself, they became personal beings, capable of exchange with other personal beings. So, as created by God, they could choose either to accept or reject the divine love.

The story of humanity must include rejection of God's love, symbolized by the fall. The first person, Adam, stands as a type of all persons in that all spurn the divine love and arrogantly assert their self-sufficiency (Rom. 3:23). Like Adam, all seek to put themselves in the place of the Creator (Gen. 3:5).

Fortunately, the Creator is not as fickle as the creature. He has never ceased his quest to woo humanity back to himself. The story of humankind—particularly of Israel, Jesus, and the church—is the story of this quest. God chose Israel to be his instrument. When Israel failed, he sought a remnant. Finally, in Jesus of Nazareth, he initiated a new humanity. As Adam had been the type of the old, now Jesus became the type of the new humanity.

As typified by Jesus, the new humanity stands in stark contrast to the old. First of all, like him, it is theocentric, obedient to God and responsive to his love. Whereas persons in the old humanity were typically self-centered, in the new humanity they are to be typically God-centered. By the grace of God, they strive for the complete openness to the divine will seen in Jesus of Nazareth. Such was exactly the call of Jesus: "If any man would come after me, let him deny himself and take up his cross and follow me" (Mark 8:34). Self-denial, of course, does not mean becoming an ascetic who rejects all contacts with the world; on the contrary, it means finding the center and focus of life in God rather than in self.

God-centeredness, in turn, will necessitate a new manner of life. The old humanity was characterized by hatred and hostility; the new humanity is characterized by *agape* love. *Agape* produces the most mature kind of interpersonal relationships. As Paul so aptly described it in 1 Corinthians 13, it replaces jealousy, boastfulness, arrogance, and rudeness with patience and kindness, placing the interests of the other person above self-interest. It applauds what is right (1 Cor. 13:4-13).

Agape is willing to go the second mile, just as God does toward his creatures. It allows no room for retaliation (Matt. 5:38-48). It asks that our manner of behavior correspond to the manner in which God has acted toward us. The one whose life is filled with *agape* pours out his life in service just as Christ did, even laying down his life for another (John 15:13).

Corporately, *agape* produces oneness within the new humanity. By his self-giving act of love, Christ put an end to the factionalism and strife of the old humanity, destroying once for all the barriers that separate person from person (Eph. 2:14). Thus, within the new humanity, "There is neither Jew nor Greek, there is neither slave nor free, there is neither male nor female; for you are all one in Christ Jesus" (Gal. 3:28). There may be natural barriers that *agape* cannot *erase*, but there are none that it cannot *transcend!* It should produce the supreme example of unity and harmony this side of the unity and harmony of Father and Son. This was, after all, Jesus' own prayer: "that they may all be one; even as thou, Father, art in me, and I in thee, that they also may be in us, so that the world may believe that thou hast sent me" (John 17:21).

Just as the new humanity is inherently one by virtue of *agape*, so also it ought to function harmoniously. It is, after all, the body of Christ. Each member should be appropriately considerate of every other member, knowing that the whole functions only as well as all of its parts. "If one member suffers, all suffer together; if one member is honored, all rejoice together" (1 Cor. 12:26).

God-centeredness should produce also the holiness characteristic of God. The word *holiness* connotes "otherness," particularly in the ethical and spiritual sense. Accordingly, the first Christians drew a distinct line between the ethical life typical of the old humanity and that of the new. Like their Jewish forebears, they made catalogs of virtues and vices to be used in instructing new converts. Paul furnished a good example in Galatians 5:19-24. "The works of the flesh," he warned, "are plain: immorality, impurity, licentiousness, idolatry, sorcery, enmity, strife, jealousy, anger, selfishness, dissension, party spirit, envy, drunkenness, carousing, and the like." By contrast, "the fruit of the Spirit is love, joy, peace, patience, kindness, goodness, faithfulness, gentleness, self-control; . . . And those who belong to Christ Jesus have crucified the flesh with its passions and desires."

The distinctiveness of this new life is sharply etched when its main features are placed alongside those of the old humanity.

The Old Humanity	*The New Humanity*
Self-centeredness	God-centeredness
Hatred toward	Love of
God	God
Fellow human beings	Fellow human beings
Discontentment	Peace
Factionalism and strife	Unity and reconciliation
Immorality or amorality	High ethical motivation

At this point, however, we must pause to confess the incompleteness of the new humanity. Because it is constituted of both human and divine elements, it does not exist in its pure form. Rather, it is overlapped in time and sphere by the old humanity.

Even within the new humanity, then, persons find themselves engaged in a perpetual struggle with their old selves. In the same way, the church must be on guard lest the old humanity dominate. If we are not careful, its defects will soon pervade the new. Whether fortunately or unfortunately, the church has not been taken out of the world but rather sent into it. Consequently, it must be on guard, lest the world squeeze it into its mold. Christians need to continually remind themselves that they are God's temple, consecrated to his service (1 Cor. 3:16 ff.; 2 Cor. 6:16; Eph. 2:21; 2 Thess. 2:4).

In spite of this threat from the old, however, the new humanity does exist. It began with the raising of Jesus of Nazareth from the dead. It continues to exist through the transmission of his life to those who have shared by faith in his death and resurrection. In some sense, then, the new humanity exists and is coming into existence at the same time. It strives, as Paul put it, to "attain to the unity of the faith and of the knowledge of the Son of God, to mature manhood, to the measure of the stature of the fulness of Christ" (Eph. 4:13). It does not claim ever to have reached its goal. But, with the Spirit's help, it continues to journey toward it.

The assurance for the new humanity, of course, stems from the fact that, although it is composed of that which is human, it is created and sustained by that which is divine. From the beginning, God has sought to gain humanity's response to his love. It is in order to accomplish this purpose that he has been at work fashioning a new humanity—in the calling of Abraham, in the making of a covenant with Israel, in the preserving of a remnant. The new humanity became a reality, however, in Jesus of Nazareth and in the Christian church. In him, "the plan of the mystery hidden for ages" was revealed at last (Eph. 3:9-10).

The new humanity, in some sense, represents the continuation of God's creative activity. Through his Spirit, God continues to create a new race. He coordinates its members to perform their appointed service in the world. He forms the nerve center that generates the mutual sensitivity and concern of its members. He instills *agape* love in it. He purifies and cleanses it (Eph. 4; 1 Cor. 12—14).

The new humanity continues the mission of Jesus Christ, but we must be careful about thinking of it as a continuation of the incarnation. The self-revelation of God in Jesus of Nazareth applies uniquely to him as head of the church. Although the church continues Christ's ministry, it should not be thought of as "Christ himself" or "another Christ" (the older Roman Catholic view), but Christ's *body*. He is "the head of the body."

So the church may not claim infallibility. Because the old humanity pervades the new, the new must undergo repeated reform and renewal at God's hands. In humility, it must seek God's forgiveness and cleansing corporately, just as do the members of the body individually (1 Cor. 5). The church must never complacently allow the old leaven to permeate the new and corrupt it.

Notwithstanding its faults, however, God has promised to sustain and preserve his church (Matt. 16:18). It has a place in God's plan for the restoration of the whole creation (Rom. 8:19). It came about through an act of his love, just as the old humanity did. Hence, we can join Paul in his triumphant refrain, sure that "neither death, nor life, nor angels, nor principalities, nor things present, nor things to come, nor powers, nor height, nor depth, nor anything else in all creation, will be able to separate us from the love of God in Christ Jesus our Lord" (Rom. 8:38-39).

The People of God

The second biblical image for the church, the people of God, furnishes the thread that unites it with Israel. At the root is the idea of a covenant made between God and a nation whom he chose for his purpose of restoring the relationship between himself and humankind. By way of explanation, let us look first at the covenant, then at the story of Israel's response to the covenant, and finally at the place of the church in the continuing story of the people of God.

According to the apostle Paul (Gal. 3:6 ff.), the covenant was made first with Abraham, whom God promised to bless and to make a blessing (Gen. 12:2). Circumcision was the seal of the covenant. The covenant was continued through Isaac, Jacob, and the twelve patriarchs. When the descendants of Jacob became enslaved in Egypt, God sent Moses to deliver them. Through Moses, he renewed his covenant, giving the Law (Ex. 19 ff.). Again and again thereafter, he repeated his pledge.

The covenant was based upon God's love (hesed). Obviously, it was an unequal agreement since it was transacted between unequal partners. In it, God became Israel's God—they became his people. He offered them sustenance and guidance—they offered him obedience or faithfulness. As long as they remained faithful to the covenant, God would always remain true to it as well: "If you will obey my voice and keep my covenant, you shall be my own possession among all peoples; for all the earth is mine, and you shall be to me a kingdom of priests and a holy nation" (Ex. 19:5-6).

On Israel's side, the moral provisions for the covenant were spelled out in an ethical code summed up in the Ten Commandments. The code consisted of two parts—the obligation to God and the obligation to fellow human beings. In essence, the two parts said, "You shall love the Lord your God with all your heart, and with all your soul, and with all your might" (Deut. 6:4) and "You shall love your neighbor as yourself" (Lev. 19:18). So vital were these that during the reign of Josiah, Israelites were commanded to carry the first in a small pouch strapped to the forehead as a perpetual reminder.

Unfortunately, Israel repeatedly broke the covenant. Scarcely had the people made their vow to do "all that the Lord has spoken" and to "be obedient" (Ex. 24:7) before they broke it in Moses' absence

(Ex. 32). Then, according to the prophets, this became typical of the nation Israel. She prostituted herself to other gods (Hosea). She did not keep her promise of moral obedience, displaying religiosity rather than righteousness (Amos). She failed to bear witness to his name, either in deed or in word (Isaiah).

Still God, whose "steadfast love endures for ever," always remained faithful. He continued to make his plea to unfaithful Israel. At last, God sought a remnant (Isa. 10:20-23). With this remnant, Jeremiah promised, he would "make a *new* covenant with the house of Israel and the house of Judah." It would be put "within them" and written "upon their hearts," not on tablets of stone. Yet his purpose would be the same: "I will be their God, and they shall be my people!" (Jer. 31:31-34).

The remnant narrowed further, according to the second Isaiah, becoming, as it were, a remnant of a remnant. Finally, according to early Christian interpretation, it had only a single representative—Jesus of Nazareth. In the minds of his followers Israel committed her final act of disobedience when she put to death this righteous one. The sons of Jacob had "received the law as delivered by angels and did not keep it" (Acts 7:53). Jesus alone remained true to Israel's covenant with God, obedient even to death.

Upon the faithfulness of Jesus of Nazareth, then, the first Christians declared, God made a new covenant in fulfillment of that foretold by Jeremiah (Rom. 11:27) and Joel (Acts 2:16-21). He was not calling a new people but transacting a new covenant with his people. They were to be no longer Israel "after the flesh" but Israel "after the Spirit" (Rom. 9:6 ff.). The death and resurrection of Jesus, the long-awaited Messiah, marked the beginning of a people of God drawn from all the nations of the earth.

It was the twelve, those chosen by Jesus himself, who formed the foundation of Israel under a new covenant, the true people of God (Rev. 21:14; Eph. 2:20). The number twelve, of course, apparently by Jesus' own design, corresponded to the number of the Old Testament patriarchs. To this foundation were added others. Finally, a host representing every nation appear as the people whom God had sought from the beginning. This story of God's quest may be diagrammed as follows:

Humanity—Israel—the Remnant—Christ—the Church—Humanity
The Old Humanity   >   +   <   The New Humanity

In the early Christian view, as Professor Oscar Cullmann has pointed out in his epochal study *Christ and Time*,[1] Christ stands at the midpoint of all history. With reference to the *past* history of Israel and even of humankind, Christ's life, death, and resurrection mean fulfillment. All that is recorded in the Old Testament points "toward the goal of the incarnation." Only as we view it from the Christ-event does it become intelligible to us. With reference to the *future* the Christ-event marks the decisive event before victory; it is the D-day before V-day. With reference to the *present*, it signifies that already the last things are taking place. We are now standing in the end time—that is, the time of God's completion of his purpose for Israel, although the last thing, the end, has not yet come. We live in the epoch between D-day and V-day.

Where does the church fit into all of this? It belongs to the last things. It is not, however, *the* last thing. *The last thing* is the consummation of the kingdom or sovereign rule of God. As the people of God, the church points to, and is the instrument of, the kingdom; but it is not to be equated with it.

It is participation in the end time that distinguishes the church as the people of God from the first Israel. In fulfillment of the prophetic hope, the Spirit that was to initiate the messianic era had now been poured out on all flesh (Acts 2:17 ff.). To the early Christian community, this confirmed conclusively Jeremiah's promise of a *new* covenant. Like "living stones" the Christians had turned to "*the* living stone," Christ, to be "built into a spiritual house, to be a holy priesthood, to offer spiritual sacrifices acceptable to God through Jesus Christ" (1 Pet. 2:5).

Because the Spirit had been poured out on all, the apostle Paul argued, race and nation no longer distinguished the people of God. Neither did circumcision or any other mark under the old covenant (Rom. 9—11). God had, as it were, grafted a wild olive branch onto the tame olive tree (11:17-24). He did this, though, in order that the tree itself might be complete and whole. His aim was the reconciliation of the world, not exclusion of the Jewish people. As the people of God, therefore, the church has become God's agent of reconciliation (2 Cor. 5:20-21). In return, God has promised his people a special blessing—they shall be to him "sons and daughters" (Matt. 5:9; Rom. 8:14 ff.; Heb. 2:10; 1 Pet. 2:1-10).

The Servant

The third image derives from Jesus' understanding of his own mission and purpose as the Servant of God. Its application to the church is, in fact, more implicit than explicit in the New Testament. In order to comprehend fully the import of it for the church, therefore, we must examine Jesus' self-understanding as revealed in his words and works, the Old Testament background for his understanding, and the implicit evidence of the concept in the early church.

If the Gospels make anything clear about Jesus' role, it is that he conceived of himself as the Servant-Messiah. Although some scholars have concluded that the early church imposed this concept in looking backwards from the cross, there is reason to believe that it originated with Jesus himself. From the beginning of his public ministry until his death on the cross, he played the role of the Servant. He even characterized himself in this way. Undoubtedly, the brief epigram that "the Son of man also came not to be served but to serve, and to give his life as a ransom for many" (Mark 10:45) reflects, to the evangelists' minds, the heart of his thinking. Let us observe this more closely in the Gospel records.

Jesus' baptism, apparently, was the point at which he intended to publicize his interpretation of his role. Difficult as it is to interpret, its meaning seems to be revealed in the words of the voice from heaven. In Mark 1:11, the words contain first a quotation from the messianic Psalm 2:7: "Thou art my beloved Son." As if by contrast, they next quote Isaiah 42:1, a Suffering Servant poem: "With thee I am well pleased." The implication is, then, that Jesus is the Messiah of the remnant, but understands his messiahship in terms of the Servant.

The temptation of Jesus confirms this interpretation. In each of the three testings recorded by Matthew (4:1-11) and Luke (4:1-13), Jesus was tempted to play the role of the Davidic messiah who would give food, perform miracles, and conquer Israel's enemies rather than be the righteous one who suffers. Each time, he resisted; he was the Servant of God.

The story of Jesus' public ministry is throughout the story of the Servant. He healed the sick, cast out demons, gave sight to the blind, cleansed the lepers, made the lame walk, forgave sinners. He reminded his detractors that he had come to minister to the sick, for those who are well do not need a doctor (Mark 2:17). So committed was he to his role as Suffering Servant that it led ultimately to his death, for his acts of compassion soon ran counter to the well-established rules.

Some time before his arrest, Jesus could already forecast his approaching death—the crowning act in the Servant's role. Three times he had to remind his disciples that "the Son of man must suffer many things" (Mark 8:31; 9:30-32; 10:32-34). Against repeated temptations, he set himself steadfastly to the accomplishment of the mission God had given. He gave a last dramatic sign in the upper room. There bread and wine affirmed in symbol that the Servant would pour out his life for many (Mark 14:24; Matt. 26:28). In the garden of Gethsemane he faced one more temptation to lay aside the Servant's yoke; then he went to the cross.

This interpretation of his role is rooted in the Old Testament understanding of God's purpose for Israel. Israel was God's son because he was his servant and conversely his servant because he was his son (Gal. 3—4). God's command delivered to Pharaoh by Moses was, "Israel is my first-born son, and I say to you, 'Let my *son* go that he may *serve* me' " (Ex. 4:22-23).

In the period of the monarchy, the terms *son* and *servant* were applied particularly to the king, who stood as the representative of Israel. David, of course, was the son and servant par excellence. Through Nathan, God had expressed his special favor to "my servant David" (2 Sam. 7:8). Not only was David himself chosen, but his lineage. At the enthronement ceremony for each new king, the king was seated on his throne with the assurance, "You are my son,/today I have begotten you./Ask of me, and I will make the nations your heritage,/and the ends of the earth your possession./You shall break them with a rod of iron,/and dash them in pieces like a potter's vessel" (Ps. 2:7-9).

After the monarchy fell, Israel's hopes turned toward the ideal king like David, the Messiah. Some continued to look for the mighty warrior who could fulfill the promise of Psalm 2:7. But at least one person, an exile, began to revive the servant image of Israel and Israel's king. In four passages, usually called the servant poems, he developed the idea fully. His thought seems to race back and forth from nation to individual. In the first poem, God speaks: He had chosen his Servant and filled him with his Spirit to bring justice to the nations (Isa. 42:1-4). In the second poem the Servant responds: He, Israel, had sought to do what God asked, but now he was discouraged. In reply, God gave further encouragement (49:1-6). In the third poem, the Servant responds once more with assurance—because the Lord God is on his side he says, "I have set my face like a flint,/and I know that I shall not be put to shame" (50:9). Finally, in the fourth poem (52:13 to 53:12), he has become the one who would pour out his life for others. "He bore the sin of many,/and made intercession for the transgressors" (53:12).

These servant poems provided the axle around which Jesus' understanding of his mission, or at least the early church's interpretation of it, turned. The Son of man was Israel's Messiah, but not of the type of David. He was rather the Suffering Servant, who came "not to be served but to serve" (Mark 10:45). As we have seen already, his baptism, the temptation in the wilderness, his brief career, and supremely his death bore witness to one fact: Jesus was the Servant chosen of God to restore the severed relationship between Israel and himself and between humanity and himself!

Appropriately, Jesus invested his followers with the same role. The calling of disciples contains warnings everywhere about the cost of discipleship. Jesus cautioned a would-be disciple that "the Son of man has nowhere to lay his head" (Matt. 8:20; Luke 9:58). He warned that his followers would share the same fate as their teacher. They would suffer exclusion from the synagogue, flogging, trial before governors and kings, and even death (Matt. 10:17-25; Mark 13:9-13; Luke 21:12-17). The disciples need not think they would escape the fate of their teacher. They would drink the same "cup" and receive the same "baptism" (Mark 10:38). In fact, being Jesus' disciple, by its very nature, entails suffering. "If any man would come after me, let him deny himself and take up his cross and follow me" (Mark 8:34).

In direct teachings, also, Jesus saw in suffering a mark of the faithful people of God. The kingdom belongs to the "poor in spirit," "those who mourn," "the meek," and "those who are persecuted for righteousness' sake" (Matt. 5:3-10). Sufferings and distress merely indicate that the prelude to the final consummation of God's purpose has begun (Mark 13).

Finally, the charges given by Jesus to the twelve and to the seventy show definitely his expectation that his disciples would play the role of servant. Like Jesus himself, they would have no earthly ties to hamper their mission. They were charged to do what he had done: "Preach as you go, saying, 'The kingdom of heaven is at hand.' Heal the sick, raise the dead, cleanse lepers, cast out demons. You received without pay, give without pay" (Matt. 10:7-8).

Although, as I remarked earlier, the early church thought of itself as servant implicitly rather than explicitly, there is abundant evidence that it did think about its role in this way. Paul reminded the Philippians, for example, that "it has been granted to you that for the sake of Christ you should not only believe in him but also suffer for his sake" (Phil. 1:29). More pointedly, he added, we ought to have in us the mind of Christ, who "emptied himself, taking the form of a servant" (Phil. 2:7).

Paul, moreover, came even nearer linking the church to the servant concept in his letter to the Colossians. "Now I rejoice in my sufferings for your sake," he declared, "and in my flesh I complete what is lacking in Christ's afflictions for the sake of his body, that is, the church" (Col. 1:24). In 1 Peter 4:12-13 we find a similar view, reminiscent of Jesus' teaching concerning persecution.

As further confirmation of the significance of the servant image in interpreting the church, Archbishop Philip Carrington has shown that the early Christian catechism included a section on submissiveness. We see it in the ethical codes in Colossians 3:18 to 4:1; Ephesians 5:21 to 6:9; Titus 3:1-7; 1 Peter 2:13 to 3:22. Citizens were to be obedient to their rulers, wives to their husbands, slaves to their masters, and children to their parents. The reason: Suffering has God's approval. "For to this you have been called, because Christ also suffered for you, leaving you an example, that you should follow in his steps" (1 Pet. 2:21).

It was undoubtedly in baptism that the servant image came forth most clearly. In baptism, one identifies fully with Christ the Suffering Servant. "All of us who have been baptized into Christ Jesus," Paul reminded those who might be tempted to slacken their moral obligations, "were baptized into his death" (Rom. 6:3). We have crucified the self, thus setting ourselves free from sin. It is through our self-renunciation and sharing in Christ's obedience that we share his triumph over death (v. 5).

This concept of the church as servant ought to make us cautious about using the oft-employed image of a church militant. The church does not exist in order to conquer its foes; God does that for it. On the contrary, it exists in order to pour out its life in service—healing the sick, casting out demons, cleansing lepers, restoring sight for the blind, providing food for the hungry, giving rest to the weary, making homes for the homeless, bringing comfort to the distraught, preaching peace to those near and far. Like Jesus himself, it lives by dying, pouring out its life to satisfy human need wherever and in whatever form it finds it. It does not strive to guarantee its own future even; rather, it lives by God's grace, seeking only to magnify him and his rule (Matt. 16:25).

The City of God

Like the image of the Servant, the fourth image, that of the city of God, was not extensively developed in New Testament writings. In the 1960s, moreover, many theologians, among them Harvey Cox, became severly critical of its use because, for many centuries, it projected "churchiness." As originally employed, however, the image depicted in a helpful way the relationship of Christianity to the world and was amply elaborated in the first several centuries. Christians saw themselves as a colony of heaven planted in the midst of an essentially alien world and charged with a responsibility to bear witness to and to transform it by being present in it.

The genesis of this image can be traced back to historical Israel. In the Old Testament era already the faithful had begun to dream of a "new Jerusalem" where justice and peace would reign. The apocalyptists of the Maccabean and post-Maccabean eras (165 B.C. and after) stated this dream in increasingly vivid images, looking always to the future. The Revelation of John set forth the apocalyptists' dream almost without alteration, a reminder that the final things are in God's hands. At the heart of the vision are the passing away of the old existence of humanity and the coming of a new under the image of "the holy city, new Jerusalem, coming down out of heaven from God, prepared as a bride adorned for her husband" (Rev. 21:2). John made clear that he shared fully the futuristic outlook of Jewish apocalyptists. But for most early writers Christian faith introduced an element of present realization in the church: The new Jerusalem, the city of God, exists already in faith if not in fact.

In the last analysis, what distinguishes the Christian from those outside the church is an intangible something drawn from participation in the Israel of God. According to the apostle Paul, "our commonwealth is in heaven" (Phil. 3:20), even while we live on earth. Possession of this citizenship means conduct compatible with the gospel of Christ (Phil. 1:27), conformable to the life of the heavenly king himself (Rom. 13:12-14). Not distinctive *customs*, such as circumcision, but distinctive *character* makes the difference. An unknown Christian apologist summed up the concept during the second or third centuries: "While living in Greek and barbarian cities as each was called and following local customs in food and clothing and other matters of life, they display the marvelous and admittedly paradoxical character of their own citizenship. They dwell in their own fatherlands, but like aliens; they share all things like citizens, but endure all things like foreigners; every foreign country is their fatherland and every fatherland a foreign country."

The writer proceeded to underline the paradoxical nature of this dual citizenship in terms of practical morality; then, in words reminiscent of Paul, he added, "They live in the flesh, but not according to the flesh. They spend their lives on the earth, but they have their citizenship in heaven . . . . They are fought by Jews like foreigners and persecuted by Greeks, and those who hate them cannot tell why they hate." [2] Alluding to 1 John, he noted that Christians are in but not of the world. "To put it shortly, what the soul is in the body, that the Christians are in the world." [3]

Behind such thinking lay the concept of a temporary sojourn or exile in the world. First Peter appealed to the readers to live exemplary lives among the Gentiles "as aliens and exiles" (1 Pet. 2:11-12), spending the time of "the alien residence" in fear of the One who judges without respect of persons (1:17). Consciousness of a *heavenly* citizenship compelled the most scrupulous behavior in recognition of the fact that "here we have no lasting city, but we seek the city which is to come" (Heb. 13:14).

The servants of God, an early second-century writer warned, should not think of preparing enduring farms and houses in this *earthly* city, governed by a foreign power, "for *your* city is far from *this* city." [4] The brilliant third-century Alexandrian biblical scholar, Origen, cited this alien status as the reason Christians could not assume public office; those who are qualified must rule over God's city, the church. By educating citizens in devotion to God, Christians do far more than the rest of humanity in making proper citizens for their fatherlands.[5]

The image of the city of God continued to develop through many centuries. It came to its fullest bloom in the fourth and fifth centuries, when the relations between church and state were no longer strained as they had been before the conversion of Constantine. The image was applied, however, in two quite distinct ways. Eusebius, bishop of Caesarea and the first church historian, and the emperor Constantine uncritically identified the city of God with the Roman Empire. Constantine, according to Eusebius, believed his victory was a victory over Satan himself. He called himself "a bishop, ordained by God to overlook whatever is external to the Church." [6]

He manifested his concern for the church, too, however, with exemptions of the clergy from certain taxes, lavish grants of land and money to the churches, the refurbishing and building of churches throughout the Empire, the removal of the capital of the Empire from Rome to Byzantium (Constantinople) in order to construct the thoroughly Christian city, and the gradual suppression of paganism. He was buried in a basilica erected in memory of the apostles, and his own coffin was placed in the midst of twelve others, depicting himself as the thirteenth apostle! The fertile imagination of Eusebius saw in all of this the beginning of the millennium. Eusebius plotted a new graph to describe the history of salvation: Abraham—Christ—Constantine. "According to the counsel of the mighty God, and through our emperor's agency," he declared on the thirtieth anniversary of Constantine's accession (335), "was every enemy, whether visible or unseen, utterly removed." [7]

Augustine, bishop of Hippo in North Africa and the most distinguished theologian of his day, presented a much more critical perspective of church and state in his classic essay on *The City of God*. He envisioned a continuous struggle between two great cities (city-states), the city of God and the earthly city. These two cities antedate even human history, originating in the division of God's angels—some ever faithful and devoted to God and others having rejected his service by choice (11.28-34). On analogy to the celestial creatures human beings likewise parted ways, beginning with the first person's disobedience and submission to the domination of the prince of fallen angels (demons), Satan (14.1 ff.).

Typified respectively by Cain and Abel, one group of persons lives according to the flesh—that is, under the devil's domination and like him (14.2-5); the other lives according to the Spirit—that is, under God's rule and with love (14.6-7). These two cities have been visible throughout human history, although the city of God has often been obscured by their intermingling (16.1 ff.). The clear and undeniable evidences of the latter began with Abraham and reached their fullness in Christ (16.12); in Abraham and his descendants God promised the calling of the Gentiles that was fulfilled in Christ and in the church (16.21 ff.).

As long as it continues on earth, however, the city of God, which consists of all the elect among angels and human beings, remains only partly visible, not completely identifiable in any earthly organization, even the church. Its citizens suffer continuous harassment from the inhabitants of the earthly city. All opposition notwithstanding, nevertheless, it proceeds steadily under God's protection to pursue its final goal of peace with God and eternal blessedness (19.13), already its possession in *hope* (19.27). At the return of Christ, after God differentiates once for all between the two cities, the saints of earth will share a resurrection to perfect communion with the devout angels and with God himself in a kingdom that has no end (19.22).

Conclusion

These four images—new humanity, people of God, servant, and city of God—contain some fertile implications about the nature and mission of the church. None is in itself adequate to express the experience of the church. Even assembled as a composite they cannot exhaust the richness of the experience. However, they will furnish us enough clues to the purpose of God for this people that we can at least begin to comprehend who we are and what we are to do.

4
The Church and the Kingdom

One of the crucial questions concerning the nature of the church is its relationship to the kingdom of God. Responses to the question have sometimes gone to opposite extremes.

On the one extreme, some have tended to equate church and kingdom, thus claiming prerogatives for the institutional church, which belongs to God alone. This tendency was observable in pre-Vatican II interpretations of the church by Roman Catholic authorities based upon the "keys" text in Matthew 16:19. It reached a peak in the high Middle Ages with Pope Boniface VIII's ridiculous assertion against rising nationalism in France, that "it is altogether necessary to salvation for every human creature to be subject to the Roman pontiff." [1] Although history has often proven the fallacy of such pretensions, the tendency to confuse church and kingdom subtly influenced the growth of Roman authoritarianism that was reaffirmed at Trent and in Vatican Council I.

A peculiar variation of this view has been the equation of the local church with the kingdom of God on earth by Landmark Baptists. The concern for absoluteness lay behind this view as well.

On the opposite extreme, others have dissociated church and kingdom completely, emphasizing religion as an individual and private matter and the church as an unwanted corruption. This was the tendency of rationalists and spiritualists of the Renaissance and Enlightenment and their heirs. Their favorite text was a mistaken rendering of Luke 17:21: "The kingdom of God is *within* you" (KJV). The phrase *within* should actually be translated *in the midst of you* (RSV), but this would not deter the devotees of private religion. They rejoiced when modern biblical criticism pointed out that Jesus had prepared and preached not the church but the kingdom. In the words of Alfred Loisy, one of the distinguished representatives of Roman Catholic modernism, "Jesus foretold the kingdom and it was the church that came." [2]

It is important to consider the issue in some detail, for both tendencies are still evident. Absolutism is still a problem in Roman Catholicism, despite the advances made by the Second Vatican Council in defining the nature of the church. Extreme individualistic tendencies, however, may be even more problematic for Protestants, as our discussion in the first chapter would indicate, for they allow no one to speak with authority—least of all the church.

The Intention of Jesus

Our understanding of the precise relationship between the church and the kingdom of God is complicated by uncertainty regarding Jesus' intention. Although some scholars—for example, Rudolph Bultmann—doubt whether we can recover Jesus' self-understanding at all, it is important to explore the issue with some care if we expect to understand whether and how the church fitted into his intention. The pressing question is: Did Jesus even leave room for the church (1) since his words preserved in the New Testament contain only two references to it (Matt. 16:18; 18:17), and those references are not considered authentic by many scholars; (2) since he seems to have expected the consummation of the kingdom within his own lifetime (Matt. 10:23)?

Jesus and the Kingdom

There can be little doubt that, in his ministry, Jesus was not preoccupied with the question of founding an institutional church such as we now know it. He was a Jew, and he discharged his mission within a first-century Jewish context. On the two occasions when he used the word *church* (in Aramaic *qahal*, in Greek *ekklesia*), assuming that Matthew recorded accurately, he would have preserved the Jewish nuance (an "assembly" of Israel without regard to size). The fact that the references appear only in Matthew, however, has caused some scholars to ask whether they were the words of Jesus or those of Matthew.

Matthew 16:18, "And I tell you, you are Peter, and on this rock

I will build my church," has long been subject to heated debate between Protestants and Roman Catholics. It could reflect the view of the church of Matthew's day, probably in Antioch, which has been put into the mouth of Jesus himself. Oscar Cullman has designated it a "post-resurrection saying" which Matthew has misplaced.[3] Matthew 18:17, which concerns procedures to be followed in a personal dispute, need not be questioned. It reflects Jesus' own situation. In this case, however, the word church clearly means a local community or assembly, one which could moderate a dispute.

Considering the difficulties posed by these two texts, it is evident that we cannot obtain direct data on Jesus' plans for the church. On the contrary, Jesus' preaching and teaching as well as his activities focused on the kingdom of God. Even here there arises the vexing question: Was the kingdom, in his mind, a wholly future or also a present reality in and through his ministry? How we answer this question has much to do with our answer regarding his intention for the church.

The former view, called *consistent* or *thoroughgoing eschatology*, was strongly argued by Johannes Weiss and Albert Schweitzer, both of whom were intent upon establishing Jesus firmly in the tradition of Jewish apocalyptists of his day. In line with Jewish eschatological thought, Schweitzer argued in his famous *Quest of the Historical Jesus* that Jesus taught in his parables that the kingdom comes automatically of its own accord. He perhaps expected the coming of the kingdom at harvesttime. The failure of this expectation to be fulfilled literally forced a change in his understanding. Because the kingdom did not come as he expected, he was compelled to suffer and die. To cite Schweitzer's graphic words,

> in the knowledge that He is the coming Son of Man [Jesus] lays hold of the wheel of the world to set it moving on that last revolution which is to bring all ordinary history to a close. It refuses to turn, and He throws Himself upon it. Then it does turn; and crushes Him. Instead of bringing in the eschatological conditions, He has destroyed them. The wheel rolls onward, and the mangled body of the one immeasurably great Man, who was strong enough to think of Himself as the spiritual ruler of mankind and to bend history to His purpose, is hanging upon it still. That is His victory and His reign.[4]

Jesus chose his disciples in order to inaugurate this movement, not to found a church.

The other view, called *realized eschatology,* was espoused with equal vigor by C. H. Dodd and T. F. Glasson, among others. Dodd contended in his study of *The Parables of the Kingdom* and other writings that Jesus did not proclaim merely the *coming* of the kingdom but that it was already here. Dodd cited particularly Matthew 12:28 and Luke 11:20: "But if it is by the Spirit [Luke has "finger"] of God that I cast out demons, then the kingdom of God has come upon you." He proceeded to argue that Jesus' basic proclamation, "The time is fulfilled, and the kingdom of God is at hand" (Mark 1:15; Matt. 4:17; Luke 10:9,11), meant that the kingdom had already arrived in Jesus himself. "John the Baptist marks the dividing line: before him, the law and the prophets; after him, the Kingdom of God." [5]

Jesus' answer to John's inquiry as to whether he was the awaited Messiah was: "The blind receive their sight and the lame walk, lepers are cleansed and the deaf hear, and the dead are raised up, and the poor have good news preached to them" (Matt. 11:5; Luke 7:22). Dodd, of course, admitted that some statements of Jesus did seem to refer to the kingdom as a future reality, the nearest to an actual prediction being Mark 9:1: "There are some standing here who will not taste death before they see the kingdom of God come with power." Of similar importance are Matthew 8:11 and Mark 14:25.

Moreover, Jesus predicted things that had no immediate reference to the kingdom of God, notably his death. These apparently contradictory phenomena can be reconciled, Dodd concluded, by recognizing that Jesus saw his own death as a part of the crisis that accompanied the presence of the kingdom in him. "This is the 'mystery of the Kingdom of God'; not only that the *eschaton,* that which belongs properly to the realm of the 'wholly other,' is now a matter of actual experience, but that it is experienced in the paradoxical form of the suffering and death of God's representative." [6]

An alternative to these two views has been propounded by Werner Georg Kümmel, among others under the rubric of *inaugurated eschatology.* Like Dodd, Kümmel too noted that Jesus' sayings included statements of both "promise" and "fulfillment." He disagreed with Dodd, however, regarding the meaning of Jesus' proclamation that "the kingdom of God is at hand" (Mark 1:15). The Greek word translated "is at hand" (*eggizein*) means not "has already arrived" but "is imminent." This would coincide with Jesus' prediction that some of those standing near him would see the kingdom of God come with power before they died (Mark 9:1). Indeed, it was so imminent that he could take a vow not to drink wine until he would drink it new in the kingdom of God (Mark 14:25).

Luke 17:21 is best translated, "The kingdom of God is present in your midst." Thus, concluded Kümmel, Jesus saw the future approach of the kingdom as already a present reality in himself. "The presence of Jesus is in itself already an eschatological hour of decision, because in *this* present, the man Jesus has appeared who confronts men with denial or confession; by their action they determine in advance the sentence of the 'Son of Man' at the final judgment." [7]

The point of this discussion is whether, as Jesus proclaimed the coming of the kingdom, he left room for the church at all. Schweitzer and the thoroughgoing eschatologists said no. Realized or inaugurated eschatologists, on the contrary, would be more likely to say yes. Jesus may have allowed some time frame before the consummation of the kingdom within which the church could function. This matter needs fuller examination.

Jesus and the Church

That Jesus did not exclude the church from his understanding of the kingdom of God can be substantiated in several ways.

First of all, as R. Newton Flew demonstrated in his excellent book *Jesus and His Church*, Jesus' conception of the kingdom of God not only made room for but necessarily implied the church. In line with Jewish thought in his day, the kingdom of God (*malkuth* Yahweh) connoted especially God's rule or reign that would be consummated in the future (Matt. 6:10) but was nevertheless now "realized" (Luke 11:20). Secondarily, Jesus gave it a territorial nuance—about entering and leaving (Mark 9:47; 10:14-15; Matt. 7:21; 16:19; 21:31; 23:13; Luke 16:16). Following from this meaning, however, is an idea of a community. The community concept is evident in Jesus' statement about John the Baptist and the kingdom. No one is greater than John, "yet he who is least in the kingdom of heaven is greater than he" (Matt. 11:11). It appears also in the parable of the mustard seed (Mark 4:30-32) and in several references by Jesus to a fellowship of believers with him in the future kingdom (Matt. 25:10,21,23,34; Mark 14:25).

Secondly, certain direct sayings and parables of Jesus reveal that, in Jesus' mind, response to the kingdom entails allegiance to him and participation in a unique experience of fellowship with the new people of God. Although many scholars question whether Jesus instructed his disciples to fast after his departure, the parables of the bridegroom and his guests, the old garment, and the old wineskins (Matt. 9:15-17; Mark 2:19-22; Luke 5:34-39) clearly signified that the old age is past and the new has arrived.

Thirdly, Jesus' calling of disciples demonstrates that he closely identified his own ministry and the kingdom of God with the forming of an eschatological community. As Eduard Schweizer demonstrated in his masterful study *Lordship and Discipleship*,[8] (1) Jesus called persons to follow him in allegiance to himself as "*the* decisive act"; (2) his calling was the beginning of something new, "an act of divine grace"; (3) following him meant "togetherness with Jesus and service to him"; (4) it entailed giving up all other ties and even one's own life; (5) as was true of Jesus himself, it led to rejection, suffering, and death and, by this way alone, to glory. In a study of *The Teaching of Jesus* T. W. Manson argued, moreover, that Jesus' instructions show a gradual narrowing of his circle of hearers. At first he addressed the crowds who followed; then he formed an inner circle; and finally he restricted his instruction to the twelve.[9]

The selection of the twelve, fourthly, offers one of the clearest evidences that Jesus integrated the church with his understanding of the kingdom. It has been argued, to be sure, that the idea of the twelve originated with the primitive church and not with Jesus himself. The chief objection is that no two lists of the names of the twelve in the Gospels and Acts agree. Evidence for the twelve, however, is very early, given by Paul as a tradition which he had himself received from others (1 Cor. 15:5; composed about A.D. 53). If authentic, the number clearly signifies Jesus' intention. As John Wick Bowman observed,[10] Jesus used this acted parable to do two things:

(a) *to teach his people that of this typical Remnant he would raise up a new congregation of Israel to displace the old one; and* (b) *to challenge, at once his own disciples, and also Israel as a whole, with the implicit, audacious claim that he had the right to do this as the Messiah of the Remnant spoken of in the prophets!*

Fifthly, Jesus' teaching, gathered in summary form in the so-called Sermon on the Mount, implies that he left room for a continuation of a community before the final consummation. The exact nature of the demands made in the Sermon, of course, have long been debated. It is doubtless best understood as an ethic of the eschatological period between Jesus' own time and the final consummation, which is impossible of human fulfillment but made possible by divine aid. In the words of A. M. Hunter, "The ethic of Jesus is an unattainable ethic which we, as his followers, are nevertheless challenged to attain." [11] No one can love as God loves (Matt. 5:43-48); yet we strive to do just that, since the age of fulfillment characterized by the coming of the Spirit upon all has now dawned (Matt. 12:28).

Finally, Jesus' fellowship meals with his disciples, concluded by what we call the Last Supper, points to the preparation of a community that would continue Jesus' activities beyond his death. Early Christian traditions differ, of course, as to whether the Last Supper was a Passover meal; and the accounts pose numerous critical problems. It cannot be doubted, however, that the meal was "*a symbol of the fellowship which will finally be the lot of those who attend the Kingdom banquet.*" [12] It pointed to Jesus' death but beyond it to his promise to share with his disciples in the great banquet of the end time.

Church and Kingdom in Tension

In the final analysis, therefore, there is ample reason to think that Jesus envisioned a relationship between the people of God as a community of the end time and the kingdom of God that was present in and through himself and his activities. Although he anticipated the consummation of the kingdom of God in the near future, perhaps in his own lifetime, he nevertheless spoke and acted at the same time on the assumption that the Father alone would decree the final hour (Mark 13:32). Through his parables—for example, the seed growing secretly and the mustard seed (Mark 4:30-32)—he warned against trying to force God's hand. The kingdom would come of its own accord (Mark 4:28). Meantime, in line with prophetic promises, he proceeded to prepare a remnant who would continue his ministry.

There is an obvious tension in Jesus' expectations of an immediate consummation of the kingdom and his own activities. The resolution of it would seem to lie in a recognition of his prophetic consciousness in which he foreshortened the time. So aware was he of what God was bringing to pass through his own life and ministry that he envisioned an immediate end. Still, that did not keep him from leaving the final answer to the Father.

Church and Kingdom in Christian Perspective

In Jesus' mind, then, the kingdom of God and the church were neither the same nor completely distinct. The community of the new age, like Jesus himself, pointed to the rule of God that was nevertheless already present in Jesus and experienceable by his followers.

The experience of the resurrection of Jesus changed the perspective of his followers in one important respect: Now they had confirmation that the age to come had indeed dawned. What John the Baptist as the Forerunner had proclaimed was now a reality. What Jesus himself announced in and through his ministry now made sense. His disciples would do even greater things than Jesus himself (John 14:12). With the resurrection of Jesus the kingdom of God had come nearer than ever for those who believed.

The first believers, however, did not make the mistake of equating the church with the kingdom of God. Indeed, Paul distinguished even the kingdom of Christ from the kingdom of God. Oscar Cullman has shown that distinctions may be made in three important facets—time, sphere, and membership.

With reference to *time* the kingdom of God is unlimited. God has created time. Both the kingdom of Christ and the church are distinguished from the kingdom of God by the fact that they are restricted to the present (inaugurated) era, while the kingdom of God, at least as Paul viewed it, alone continues in the future. The

Christian now stands in the kingdom not of God but of Christ. This will become the kingdom of God at a future time (1 Cor. 15:23 ff.). Christ's reign began at the resurrection and ascension and will end with his return.

In the Revelation (20:1-6) the millenial kingdom will be included also in Christ's reign, extending beyond the period of the present to the future aeon. So also the church. "The millennium will be the Church of this final phase." [13] Thus the church shares in the same tension between present and future that the kingdom of Christ does. Because it possesses the Spirit, it belongs to the age-to-come (Acts 2:17 ff.). But it possesses the Spirit only as an "earnest" (2 Cor. 2:22) or "firstfruits." Therefore, it waits for the time when God becomes "all in all" (1 Cor. 15:28).

With reference to *sphere* the kingdom of God is again unlimited. Viewed in terms of the ancient conception of a three-storied universe, it encompasses all things in heaven, on earth, and under the earth. God's rule knows no boundaries. The kingdom of Christ is likewise unlimited with respect to sphere. As a gift of the Father, Christ possesses "all authority . . . in heaven and on earth" (Matt. 28:18). But Christ's rule is not as comprehensive as the kingdom of God in its effect until the end. Christ exercises his sway in the period between D-day (the cross) on which he dealt the forces of evil a fatal blow and V-day (his return) when the powers of evil will be finally bound and then destroyed. Presently he rules over the state through intermediaries (Rom. 13:1-7). One day, however, "at the name of Jesus every knee should bow, in heaven and on earth and under the earth" (Phil. 2:10). He will reconcile all things, "whether on earth or in heaven" (Col. 1:20).

By way of contrast, the church is confined to the strictly earthly sphere of the kingdom. This, however, does not mean it is inconsequential. Because of its submission to Christ as its head, it is "the heart and centre of the *Regnum Christi*," [14] as the phrase "the body of Christ" signifies. Being the body of Christ puts the church in a paradoxical situation. On the one hand, it experiences the suffering of Christ in the flesh. In Paul's words, "in my flesh I complete what is lacking Christ's afflictions for the sake of his body, . . . the church" (Col. 1:24). In baptism each Christian "dies with Christ" (Rom. 6:3

ff.). The lot of members of the body is the same as that of its Lord (Mark 10:38-39).

On the other hand, the body of Christ experiences also Christ's resurrection and exaltation. Christ is "the first-born among many brethren" (Rom. 8:29). To be sure, the church experiences these things only as a "foretaste" of God's final plan for humankind. Through the gift of the Spirit, nevertheless, it has a clear hope. Despite human limitations, it expects to attain to "the oneness of the faith and knowledge of God's son, to perfect manhood, to the measure of the stature of Christ's fulness" (Eph. 4:13).

In this context two passages of Scripture, those concerning binding and loosing (Matt. 16:19; 18:18), merit special mention. The debate about their authenticity was noted earlier. Both passages imply that the church's authority in matters of discipline extends not merely throughout the earthly but even to the heavenly realm. Older Protestant efforts to say that these words applied only to the kingdom were rather strained. The "keys" allude to the authority of a king's chamberlain to open the city gates (Isa. 22:15 ff.). Peter is Christ's chamberlain. The sense of both statements is that the church on earth carries out "heaven's decisions, communicated by the Spirit," and not that heaven confirms whatever the church decides.[15] The original context of the statement about binding and loosing would have been rabbinic interpretation and application of the Law. As the revealed will of God, the Law would have had divine sanction.

With reference to *membership,* the kingdom of God and/or the kingdom of Christ are all-inclusive. They embrace even "principalities and powers" above or below the earth. Even though some do not acknowledge Christ's rule, all still are subject to it. Even the government of a state belongs to this kingdom. Christians "render to Caesar the things that are Caesar's" (Mark 12:17) not because a ruler possesses anything of himself but because he acts as God's steward and instrument. They obey the powers that be because "they are ordained of God" (Rom. 13:1 ff.). The church, on the contrary, consists only of those who *acknowledge* Christ's rule. By this acknowledgment the church takes a very important place in the purpose of God. It stands at the very center of the kingdom of Christ. In this sense the members "reign together with Christ" (2 Tim. 2:12) and continue his struggle with the rulers of this world.

It should be pointed out that, in early Christian perspective, the kingdom or rule of God is experienced in different ways according to the response given to it. To those who reject God's claims upon them, the kingdom is experienced as judgment. To those who accept them, it is experienced as redeeming love. According to John 3:17-19, God did not send the Son to condemn but to save the world. Those who believe, therefore, do not experience condemnation. But those who deny are self-condemned because, when the Light came into the world, they rejected it, thus aligning themselves with the forces of darkness.

The Task of the Church

From the preceding discussion it should be evident that the church is neither the same as the kingdom nor completely separate from it. On the one hand, it is differentiated from the kingdom of God with reference to time, sphere, and membership, and from the kingdom of Christ with reference to sphere and membership. On the other hand, the church has been given a very important role in relation to God's rule. In its own life it continually shows forth the kingdom of God. It seeks to be truly Christ's body. It proclaims the good news of the kingdom. It extends an invitation to all humanity to share in the good news. It pours out its life in service just as Christ did. However, it can never forget that it points to something beyond itself. It belongs to the last things, but it is not itself *the* last thing. The last thing is the kingdom of God and his righteousness.

5
The Church and the World

On the opposite pole from the question of the church's relationship to the kingdom of God stands that of its relationship to the world. At this pole the pressing issue is: How does the church maintain its sense of identity while discharging what it understands to be its mission in and to the world? Culture—what human beings do with nature—possesses, as all recognize, a powerful molding force. It can readily squeeze individuals, groups, and institutions within a certain society into its mold (Rom. 12:2). Beginning at infancy, it generates images of belief and creates patterns of behavior for those who participate in it. Some sociologists consider it determinative of all behavior and belief.

To a considerable extent, cultural induction is beneficial and essential. No individual and no group within a society could function meaningfully and contribute significantly to it without indoctrination in its ways. The aim of education, at least in part, is to equip members of a particular society to understand, to appreciate, to fit into, and to contribute to that culture. Hopefully, education will conserve and pass on the more worthy elements of culture and will assist members of a society to find new elements as a society progresses.

However, cultural induction also poses problems. It may do its work so well that both individuals and groups become pawns of the culture, unable to differentiate between values and priorities that are handed down. Christianity, like other religions, has not escaped this dilemma. At times it, too, in its institutional expression, has become little more than an echo of culture and has rubber stamped whatever the culture produced. Identified so completely with the culture, it has had little of significance to offer.

Through the centuries Christians have adopted varied attitudes toward culture. These attitudes range across a spectrum from strong criticism and even opposition to gullible toleration and even complete approbation. A review of alternative approaches will assist in the formulation of our own position.

Separationism

On one end of the spectrum is a clam approach. Ideally radical exponents of this view would put Christianity in a ghetto, isolated entirely from the world, which is seen as the realm wholly dominated by forces of evil. Normally, however, they have had to make certain concessions to the fact that the church always lives in the world even when it does not wish to be of it.

The stricter form of this attitude is not found in the New Testament, although the persecution situation addressed by the seer of the Revelation forced him in this direction. The author of 1 John, however, opted for a definitely negative and critical attitude toward the world—that is, everything outside the church. "Do not love the world or the things in the world," he commanded. "If any one loves the world, love for the Father is not in him" (2:15). The world is characterized by "the lust of the flesh and the lust of the eyes and the pride of life," such things as are opposed to God's will.

Moreover, the world is temporary, destined to pass away (2:16-17). Christ came "to destroy the works of the devil," who rules the world (3:8). The Christian, one "born of God," does not let the world gain control but "overcomes the world" (5:4). The author did not comment on Christian attitudes to social institutions or government. Perhaps, as H. Richard Niebuhr observed, anticipating the end of the world in the immediate future, he demanded "loyalty to Jesus Christ and to the brotherhood, without concern for the transitory culture." [1]

One of the better-known exponents of this view was Tertullian of Carthage, a lawyer converted to Christianity about A.D. 195, who later joined the early Pentecostal-type Montanist sect. As a Catholic, he forbade attendance at the shows and games of the circus, theater, or amphitheater. Nothing so sets Christians apart from pagans as nonattendance, he explained, "and so he openly 'denies' who takes away that by which he is known." [2] He denounced the wearing of gaudy apparel, jewelry, cosmetics, and wigs, and the dyeing of hair by women. Christian women should differ from pagan even in the way they walk.

As a Montanist, he perhaps sharpened some of the lines of separation, though it would be difficult to ascertain how much. In writings of the Montanist period he forbade wearing of the laurel wreath, military service, any occupation connected with astrology and magic, teaching in public grammar schools, participation in pagan celebrations (unless private), placing wreaths in heathen temples, and wearing the purple toga. Though he tolerated continued contacts between Christians and pagans, he warned about letting down one's guard. Christians have to *live* with pagans, but they don't have to *sin* with them!

The critical spirit of Tertullian was later incorporated into the sectarian and also the monastic spirit and outlook. Besides the Montanists, the Novatianists and Donatists likewise repudiated the world and sought a pure church, free of cultural entanglements. It was monasticism, however, which embodied an antiworldly (*contemptus mundi*) philosophy most fully.

Adding fuel to the flames was a conviction that matter is evil, a view that captured the popular mind in the last century or more of the Roman Empire. Many bright and devout youths fled the decaying civilization and sought the solitude of the desert, where they could carry on a battle against the power of evil. They were athletes and soldiers of Christ, intent on showing contempt for the world and its vices. Although the negative stance moderated some with the passing of time, the early hermit epitomized the most radical forms of renunciation. Simeon Stylites (d. 459), to cite one specimen, perched atop a pillar in the desert of Syria laden with chains for more than thirty years. His asceticism eloquently enunciated the monastic rejection of the world.

The Renaissance signaled the end of the predominantly otherworldly outlook and the beginning of a more this-worldly one. Protestant reformers, for varied reasons, closed monasteries. Even in Protestantism, nevertheless, the more critical "Christ-against-culture" spirit of monasticism lived on in radical reformers such as the Anabaptist. The insistence of Anabaptists upon clear separation from the world would now appear to be traceable to monasticism, which supplied Anabaptism many of its eminent converts. The *Hutterite Chronicle* said that Manz, Grebel, and Blaurock, the founders of Swiss Anabaptism, called for "separation from the world and its evil works." [3]

This same critical spirit persisted in various radical groups after the Reformation, including English Puritans. The Puritans took great offense at such things as statuary, stained-glass windows, or other ornamentation as evidences of idolatry. As heirs of the Puritans, Baptists and Quakers have leaned in the direction of the puritan negation of culture.

The direct descendants of the Anabaptists and conservators of their critique of culture, however, are the Mennonites. Among Mennonites, the Old Order Amish, at considerable cost to themselves, have maintained the strictest stance. Though other Mennonites, even other Amish, draw church-culture lines most Protestant groups do not, the Old Order Amish live in virtual cloistered seclusion. They subsist by farming, refusing to use modern agricultural conveniences such as electricity, tractors, and mechanized equipment. They have repeatedly done battle with state laws that require education of their children past the eighth grade or those that require the use of safety reflectors on horse-drawn equipment. Recently some Amish farmers in Indiana have sold their dairy cattle rather than accede to milk regulations that would require them to purchase milk-cooling equipment in order to lower the temperature of the milk within a brief span of time.

Syncretism

On the opposite extreme from the preceding approach is a sponge approach—a more or less complete accommodation to culture. For the most part proponents of this view have argued for accommodation out of concern for making Christianity comprehensible and attractive to the masses. Often they have accommodated subconsciously rather than consciously but nevertheless decisively.

In the New Testament one can already discern trends in this direction as Christianity struggled to free itself from strict ties to Judaism in order to pursue the mission to the Gentiles. To many Jewish Christians, of course, discarding such marks as circumcision represented so radical a break as to cause a loss of identity. Even the twelve wrestled cautiously with this matter, as the early chapters of Acts show. It was the martyr Stephen and then the apostle Paul, however, Jews of Hellenistic background, who opened the way for substantial accommodation with a view to winning the Gentiles.

Although Niebuhr has classified Paul in the category "Christ and Culture in Paradox," it is difficult not to recognize that the apostle prepared for extensive cultural accommodation. In his defense of his apostolate to the Gentiles he expressed a principle that implies radical accommodation. "I have become all things to all men, that I might by all means save some" (1 Cor. 9:22). He argued too, that "Christ is the end of the law, that every one who has faith may be justified" (Rom. 10:4) and denounced those who attempted to impose Jewish ritual customs on his Gentile converts. To return to Jewish legalism would be to fall from grace (Gal. 5:4).

Lest it seem that Paul placed no limit on cultural accommodation out of eagerness to win all, however, we must hasten to observe Paul's own vehement denials. He repeatedly recalled his converts to observance of ethical codes taken from both Jewish and Hellenistic sources. By virtue of faith, he contended, Christians are free. Freedom in Christ, however, does not mean moral license, doing whatever one wishes. By virtue of love the Christian will not merely discharge but even go beyond the requirements of the law (Rom. 13:8-10). Love will give a sense of things that really matter (Phil. 1:10); it will supply critical discernment.

The critical element seen here in Paul often got lost in actual practice, even among Paul's converts. One may observe in the Corinthian community, for example, that some missed the responsibility side of Paul's teaching, interpreting him as saying, "Anything goes!" One convert, for instance, could not see the wrong in an incestuous relationship with his stepmother (1 Cor. 5:1-8); others could not decide what to do about eating meat slaughtered in connection with pagan rites (1 Cor. 8:1-8; 10:1 to 11:1).

In the second century there appeared numerous proponents of radical accommodation, usually labeled Gnostics. The Gnostics varied widely in their views, as modern scholarship is demonstrating more and more forcefully. At least one sect, the Valentinians, was intensely missionary and, for that reason, used every means to make Christianity intelligible and attractive to the cultured of their day. In doing so, they by no means thought that what they were doing was heretical. Valentinus tried to explain Christianity in terms of the prevailing philosophy of the early second century, Platonism. In their eagerness to align Christianity with Platonism the Gnostics had to come to terms with the Old Testament Scriptures. They did so in different ways. Some rejected it entirely as the work of an inferior deity. Others, like Ptolemaeus, a disciple of Valentinus, followed in the steps of Philo, a great Jewish apologist in the first century.

Ptolemaeus divided the Law into three parts—one from God himself, the second from Moses, the third from the elders of the people. He subdivided the first part into three additional parts: (1) "the pure legislation which is unmixed with evil," which Jesus referred to in Matthew 5:17; (2) that mixed with evil and unrighteousness which he came utterly to destroy (for example, the *lex talionis*); and (3) "the typical and symbolic, patterned after the image of the spiritual and transcendent, which the Savior transformed from perceptible and phenomenal into spiritual and invisible" (sacrifices, circumcision, sabbath, passover, unleavened bread).[4]

Through its many centuries of existence Christianity has frequently veered toward the sponge approach, especially in the centuries after Constantine when, in both East and West, the state was willing to enter into an alliance. Christians of the fourth century can be forgiven surely for rejoicing in the cessation of persecution, perhaps even for dampening their critical spirit toward Graeco-Roman culture. Sometimes, however, they let their enthusiasm run away with them, as we saw earlier in looking at Eusebius' and Constantine's concept of the city of God. "Surely it must seem to all who duly regard these facts," Eusebius wrote, "that a new and fresh era of existence had begun to appear, and a light heretofore unknown suddenly to dawn from the midst of darkness on the human race."[5]

It is always difficult to say who influenced whom the most in the holy alliance—church or empire. Christianization no doubt took place, but so did extensive accommodation. In the West the church, influenced by Augustine's thought, remained more critical of culture, though it too came dangerously close at times to equating Christ with culture. It was this that in the nineteenth century led the Danish philosopher Kierkegaard to launch an attack on Christendom in his native land. Since Kierkegaard's day, we have been witnessing the breakup of Christendom and the edging out of religion in western society. Recognition of this fact has led to a curious new proposal about the accommodation of Christianity.

During the 1960s some theologians called for an abandonment of the churches' sheltered sanctuaries and an embracing of secularity. Harvey Cox, by no means the most extreme exponent of this view, lauded the shape and the style of the secular city—anonymity, mobility, pragmatism, and profanity. Anonymity allows freedom to choose one's friends. Rather than opposing it, the churches should "develop a viable theology of anonymity." Although high mobility does "play havoc with traditional religion," Cox insisted that Christians should not resist it but recover the concept of God's mobility.

Pragmatism, the tendency to choose what works, likewise can be adopted. "There is no necessary contradiction between the biblical view of truth and that which is emerging in our functional society," concluded Cox.[6] Thence, while we will not get locked in on pragmatism as a world view, we should not resist its operation. Finally, profanity, that is, this-worldliness, is a liberating feature of secularization that deserves fully to be adopted. The church's task is to advance the process of secularization, not to retard it.

Synthesis

Three alternative positions strike the spectrum somewhere between these two extremes. One proposes a synthesis of Christianity and culture. A second emphasizes the paradox between them. A third works toward the transformation of culture.

Synthesis was scarcely conceivable for Christianity at the beginning. There were not many cultured and well-educated persons becoming Christians. By the mid-second century, however, that situation had begun to change. Thence Justin of Rome tried to demonstrate that Christianity was the true philosophy, combining the best of Hellenistic and Jewish thought. Wherever truth appeared, it was inspired by the divine Word who came in the flesh in Jesus. It remained for Clement of Alexandria, however, to articulate the position more precisely as a growing number of cultured persons manifested interest in Christianity.

Clement saw both Jews and Greeks as tutors leading to Christ. The divine Word, the universal Reason, inspired the Hebrew prophets and the Greek wise men and philosophers. If one were to make a collage of all the scraps of wisdom found in both, he or she would find the truth. The Word, however, became incarnate in Jesus Christ. He, therefore, is *the* Teacher. In line with this basic understanding, Clement was prepared to accept truth wherever he found it. Accordingly, he accepted a Platonic world view and Stoic ethical thought as quite amenable to Christianity. His rule of thumb for Christian life-style was moderation.

In contrast to Tertullian, with his emphasis on distinctive behavior, Clement depicted the Christian as a true gentleman or gentlewoman guided in all things by moderation and propriety. They should eat simple foods in moderate amounts, drink wine in moderation and with proper manners, furnish their homes usefully rather than ostentatiously, avoid revelry at parties and banquets, be "pleasantly witty, but not clownish," and avoid indecent talk and sights. Both men and women should follow the principle of moderation in dress, adornments, style, and general conduct.

Another attempt at synthesis of thought occurred in the high Middle Ages. Following Clement, Christian thinkers, especially Augustine, had achieved a kind of uneasy union between Christianity and Neoplatonism, the prevailing philosophy of the early centuries. This union, however, began to be challenged as Aristotle became better known in the West again through contacts with Jewish and Arab philosophers. A new synthesis, including Aristotle, was put together by the "schoolmen." It reached its finest expression in Thomas Aquinas. In Aquinas, however, the synthesis was most successful on the philosophical side, for Aquinas placed Christ far above culture and was himself a monk. He actually wanted culture dominated by the church.

Dualism

Approaching the separationist position is one that maintains a tension between Christianity and culture. One may see distinct evidences of this view, along with others, in Paul's writings. Paul spoke of a Christian citizenship. On the one hand, Christians were citizens of the Roman Empire and thus needed to be mindful of their obligations. They were to obey the established authorities, recognizing that God had ordained them (Rom. 13:1-7).

In his mission work Paul evidently came increasingly to value order and taught his converts to respect it. Slaves should obey their master and children their parents. Wives should voluntarily submit to their husbands. youths should respect their elders. Freedom in Christ did not give a license for disorder (Col. 3:18 to 4:1; Eph. 5:22 to 6:9; 1 Tim. 5:1-2). On the other hand, Paul spoke of a heavenly citizenship (Phil. 3:20). He urged his converts to behave in a manner that befitted this citizenship and not merely an earthly one (Phil. 1:27). Alluding to Jesus' teaching, he taught them to differentiate between God's and Caesar's realm. In cases where conflict occurred, they should obey God rather than human beings.

A similar point of view appeared in an anonymous apology for Christianity during the second or third century. The author of the *Epistle to Diognetus* observed that "the distinction between Christians and other persons is neither in country nor language nor customs" (5.1). Christians live in the same cities, speak the same language, and, for the most part, observe the same customs. While doing so, however, "they show forth the wonderful and confessedly strange character of the constitution of their own citizenship" (5.4). This means that they live as aliens in their own fatherland and can accept any foreign country as their own. "To put it shortly what the soul is in the body, that the Christians are in the world" (6.1).

That is, they are in the world but not of it. They dwell among corruptible things, "waiting for the incorruptibility which is in heaven" (6.7). The anonymous author, however, held certain opinions that led him beyond the dualist view to the conversionist. Christians, he argued, have a mission to the world. "God has appointed them to so great a post, and it is not right for them to decline it." (6.1).

Dualist thought of this type came to expression many times subsequently. In the Middle Ages it represented the mainstream of western Christian thinking about church-state relations until the schoolmen worked out a kind of synthesis. The synthesis broke down in the Protestant Reformation, however; and the major reformers, especially Luther, returned again to the dualist model.

Caught in a swirl of controversies that accompanied the Protestant Reformation, Luther himself epitomized the paradox he saw in the human situation. He, for example, could both issue a call for the freedom of the Christian and exhort the German princes to "stab, smite, slay like mad dogs the murderous and rapacious hordes of peasants." He recognized the importance of culture and supported the development of liberal-arts education in German Protestant universities. At the same time he also had reservations, for he recognized also the strength of human self-love. Only the grace of God could set human beings free from self-love. Christ cleanses the springs of action and re-creates the community in which all action takes place. He sets persons free from special vocations and calls them into pious service of their neighbors, not in monasteries and conventicles but in the world.

Roger Williams, the first Baptist in America, gave expression to this same view in his insistence upon the radical separation of church and state. Through him the dualist position has exerted a powerful influence on American thought.

Conversionism

The final perspective of the relationship between church and culture stands in the center of the spectrum. It is characterized chiefly by a concern for conversion of culture as well as conversion of individuals. Like the dualist view described above, it emphasizes the sinful nature of human beings and the consequent corruption of culture. But, unlike the former, it has confidence that culture can be transformed. It has confidence that the power of good will triumph in the end over the power of evil.

Conversionist thought pervades much of the Bible. It is clearly implied in the central biblical motif of eschatological salvation. God's purpose is not only to save individuals but even more to save humanity. According to the servant poems in Isaiah (49:6), it was for this reason that God called Israel—to be "a light to the nations." In New Testament writings the same perspective comes through even more clearly. His dualism notwithstanding, the apostle Paul represented a conversionist view as well. He would have nothing to do with the tendency of some to see no good in created things or in human culture. Even the creation, he remarked, is experiencing the birth pangs that prefigure redemption (Rom. 8:22 ff.). As long as we await the consummation, we are to be engaged in Christ's redemptive activity, doing all that we do to the glory of God, each in his/her particular calling (1 Cor. 7:17-24).

The clearest conversionist thought, as H. Richard Niebuhr pointed out, appears in the Gospel according to John. John, even allowing for the dualism of his flesh-spirit and darkness-light motifs, left no doubt about the positive implications of God's redeeming act in Christ. The Word, through whom God created the world, became flesh and dwelled among us (1:14). This means that "God so loved the world that he gave his only Son, that whoever believes in him should not perish but have eternal life. For God sent the Son into the world, not to condemn the world, but that the world might be saved through him" (3:16-17). In John *world* can at times designate the fallen order, that ruled by Satan; but John in no way agreed with the Gnostic judgment that the material is evil. The important thing is that the world is the object of redemption even when it rejects the Son.

A similar perspective lay behind the thought of later Christian theologians such as Augustine, John Calvin, and John Woolman. Augustine reflected several emphases in his writings, including the opposite extremes of monastic opposition to culture and Neoplatonic synthesis of culture and Christianity. Nevertheless, his basic theological outlook, his career, and his influence on later Christianity fit the conversionist scheme. On the basis of his own experience, Augustine was convinced that Christ would regenerate and vivify human life, which presently is corrupted on account of the fall and lies under the curse of transiency and death. He concluded the *Confessions* with a hymn of praise for conversion. "Thou, O God, savest everything that thou hadst made, and, behold, it was very good. Yea we also see the same, and, behold, all things are very good." [7]

Jesus Christ came, Augustine insisted, not only to heal each person's perverted nature but also to restore culture. He rebuked pride, detached us from self-love, revealed God's love, and reattached us to the good. This process has an impact on all human behavior, including mathematics, logic, natural science, the fine arts, and technology. Living in a time of the collapse of civilization, however, Augustine did not envision a temporal fulfillment of his ideal city of God. That lay always beyond history. Augustine thus ended with a dualism more radical than Paul's, but his more positive outlook had a powerful effect in shaping medieval Christendom.

Calvin's thought is so similar to Augustine's that it does not need further comment here. More unequivocally conversionist was the American Quaker John Woolman. Although he left no extensive legacy of writings to explain his rationale, his career and influence bear eloquent testimony about it. In his Journal he records how, at about age twenty-one, he developed pangs of conscience when he had to write a bill of sale for a black female slave. He vowed never again to repeat that deed. Instead, he felt the leading of God to travel at his own expense around the American colonies to plead with Quakers to free their slaves. So strong was his conviction that he limited his own business lest he become too immersed in worldly pursuits to do God's bidding. He wore unbleached muslin suits because the dye used in dyeing men's clothing was made from indigo, a product of slave labor. Largely as a consequence of his efforts, after 1787 no American Quaker owned a slave.

Which Way Today?

The preceding discussion should place in bas relief the varied Christian responses to the issue of church and world. Considered from the perspective of the mission of the church, each of the five views possesses both strengths and weaknesses.

The *separationist* approach potentially allows a clear witness of the Christian idea, but the separation makes questionable how most of the world's peoples will see, learn from, and respond to it. Christianity, moreover, is never detachable from cultural expression. Separation results in a normativizing of an older culture that heightens the problem of communication by virtue of its alien character. The Old Order Amish, for example, conserve seventeenth-century Swiss culture, not a uniquely Christian one.

By way of contrast, the *syncretist* approach opens the way for maximum acceptability to persons living in a certain culture. There is little or no cultural gap. The problem that this approach poses, however, is one of Christian identity. What does the church have to offer that the culture does not possess already? In the present setting, for example, merely to affirm modern secularity would do nothing but add to the problems persons in the technological culture of the West already have, for the inadequacies of this culture are becoming manifest in a series of crises—energy, ecology, food, and many more. In order to offer a constructive alternative, the church must retain a sense of identity over against culture.

The *synthesist* approach lessens to some extent the severe difficulty of identity seen in the syncretist approach. Indeed, the aim is the creation of a *Christian* culture. The difficulty with this approach is a practical one, implementation. Something like a Christian culture has existed, of course; but it depended on an alliance between church and state, which always remained very tenuous. In the East this alliance took the form of a dominance of the church by the state. In the West it resulted in bitter struggles between church and state as the church sought to exercise influence without submitting to state dominance. In both instances religious liberty suffered, even with Protestant models. What history has shown is that a "Christian" state, Christendom, is a very elusive phenomenon. The city of God lies beyond history. We strive to attain it, but it eludes our reach.

The dualist approach is more realistic than the synthesist approach. Its stress on the fallenness not only of individuals but of society as well averts the illusion of a kingdom of God on earth while not giving up completely on society. It thus obviates the extreme anti-worldly stance of the separationist approach. The difficulty it presents is that it tends to discourage or at least to de-emphasize concern for society, due to skepticism about its reformability.

Of the five approaches the *conversionist* seems to have the most in its favor. It combines the realism of the dualist approach with the optimism of the synthesist approach in such a way as to generate a motive for social transformation without falling into a utopianist trap. As a consequence, social concern is tempered by realism. To use Augustine's phrasing, we strive after the city of God, which nevertheless lies always beyond history. The ultimate goal is achieved not by human effort but by divine design.

6
The Church and the Churches

A matter of no small concern to Christians is how to interpret the crazy-quilt pattern of religious groupings that make up the religious map of the world today. A few years ago, most Christians looked at the issue in terms of relationships between Protestants. Some recent developments, however, have changed the issue dramatically. First the Orthodox and then Roman Catholics became involved in the once exlusively Protestant ecumenical movement. These events broadened the question to: How do all Christians express their essential unity? Almost simultaneously with this development, a series of world crises shifted the ecumenical question completely. Christians began asking: How do we express our unity with all human beings? How can all persons of goodwill join together to confront the crises of our time? The resultant trend has been from confrontation to dialogue.

Persons who belong to a conservatively oriented denomination such as the Southern Baptist Convention may find such trends disturbing. The growth of pluralism in America, as in the rest of the world, however, will not allow serious persons to avoid framing a position on the subject. In the past two decades we have witnessed not merely the growth of Christian sects in America but the importation and development of all kinds of sects, many with Oriental roots. As a result, the tolerance level has lifted, so that even conservative Christians are less likely to claim absoluteness for their particular expression of Christianity, as they once did, and more likely to credit other sects with some merit. Meantime, dialogue between persons of varied faiths is going on nearly everywhere.

Against this background this chapter will grapple with some of the issues raised first about the relationship between Christian denominations and then about the relationship of Christianity to other religions. In some respects the questions posed by these relationships are similar, in other cases quite different.

Inter-Christian Relationships

It is evident that inter-Christian relationships have experienced a violent change in the past two decades, specifically since John XXIII became pope in 1958. Prior to that date, the so-called ecumenical movement was strictly an effort of Protestants to express their unity with one another through cooperation, conversation, and union. Though Roman Catholics had gotten frequent invitations to participate in such ecumenical ventures as the World Council of Churches, they regularly declined them. John XXIII singlehandedly turned the ecumenical tide, however, by speaking of Protestants as "separated brothers" rather than heretics, encouraging visits to Rome by Protestants, sending Roman Catholic observers to the assembly of the World Council of Churches at New Delhi, and, above all, convening the Second Vatican Council. One of the express aims of the Council was the improvement of relationships between all Christians. Catholics have seriously followed up on this aim through cooperation in joint endeavors, dialogue, and occasionally joint worship with Protestants and Orthodox.

One fear that many Protestants, particularly Baptists, have often expressed about the ecumenical movement, even before Rome entered the picture, is that its exponents sought a "super church." The entrance of Rome may only have heightened their apprehensions, for the history of Roman Catholic authoritarianism is a matter of record. These fears have been mitigated to some degree by the fact that, since Vatican II, Roman Catholics have disproven the widely held Protestant theory of a monolithic unity by a display of pluralism, but they have not been laid to rest once for all. The current authority crisis in the Roman Church raises anew some of the long-debated questions about Rome's ultimate intentions.

"That All May Be One"

Whatever we may conclude about the ecumenical movement, we are likely to be torn between biblical statements about the oneness of the church, whether considered as a local congregation or as the people of God throughout the world, and the actuality that we see. Although some dispute whether Jesus actually spoke the words, there seems to be little question that Jesus' "high priestly" prayer that his disciples "may be one even as we are one" (John 17:22) represented Jesus' intention.

The point is driven home with equal force in Paul's analogy of the church as the body of Christ. In response to those who divided the Corinthian church by pride in spiritual gifts, the apostle cited the body metaphor. As the human body, though composed of many and diverse members, functions as a single unit, so also should Christ's body, the church. No member, however insignificant, is to be neglected or forgotten (1 Cor. 12:12-26). Love is the perfect bond that will unite the diverse members (Col. 3:14). There is "one body and one spirit, . . . one hope . . . one Lord, one faith, one baptism, one God and Father of all" (Eph. 4:4-6). We all strive to attain to "the unity of the faith and the knowledge of God's Son to perfect humanity to the measure of the stature of Christ's fulness" (4:13). In other words, we grow up into Christ, the head of the body, the church, through whom God has sought to reconcile all things (Col. 1:18, 20).

The actuality is quite different. The one body of Christ does not appear unified. It is divided, rather, into a multiplicity of sects and denominations, nearly three hundred in the United States alone. Although these groups often carry on dialogue or cooperate, they certainly lack functional and structural oneness. In some instances, as a matter of fact, they deny the validity of other groups besides themselves. The actuality thus poses a serious question about divisions in relation to the reality of Christ's body.

The Nature of Schism

For many centuries it has been customary for Christians to interpret division or schism as separation from the true body of Christ. Thus each denomination claimed to be the true representative of Christianity, and other denominations or sects branches were to be lopped off and deserving of destruction. Catholics, for example, claimed that the reformers split off from the one true church. The reformers countered by arguing that the Roman Church invalidated itself by allowing corruption. By excommunicating the reformers, it severed itself from the true Catholic church. Thus the Protestant churches replaced the early church as the true representative of Christ. One schismatic group after another honed the same argument.

In recent years ecumenical discussion has produced a different attitude and outlook. In a study of *Schism in the Early Church,* S. L. Greenslade [1] proposed that we think of schism as occurring *within* and not *from* the church. No person or group who believes in Christ can be separated from his body, the church. Such separation could occur only where a group denied Christ—that is, by heresy. It could not result from differences of opinion about church order or discipline. To be sure, divisions may occur *within* the one body. These are grievous and distressing, and an effort should be made to heal such breaches. But this is not a matter of branches lopped off and restored. Rather, it involves a process of internal injury and repair.

The Nature of the Unity Sought

This brings us to the crucial question: Given the state of division that exists within the body of Christ, what is the nature of the unity we should seek? Several answers have been seriously proposed.

Some persons would simply acknowledge a *spiritual unity* of Christians, seeing no serious reason for efforts to obtain organizational or participatory unity. They often stress, quite rightly, the manifest contributions of diverse denominations to the spread of Christianity in America. Competition has proven to be a stimulus to growth; and, some would argue, only weak or dying denominations want to join others. Denominationalism is essentially good, therefore.

The question that has to be asked of exponents of this view, however, is: Granting the benefits of diversity, is spiritual unity what Christ intends for his church? Or does he wish more? Moreover, one must ask also to what extent divisions and competition may have impeded as well as aided the growth of churches. Have they not caused perplexity and sometimes rejection of Christianity? This certainly has been true on foreign mission fields, where prospective converts have often wanted to know which group really represented

Christ. Accordingly, it is not surprising that the ecumenical movement got its start out of concern for the world mission enterprise,
the famous Edinburgh conference of 1910 usually being pinpointed
as the take-off point.

Other persons would go to the opposite extreme and argue for
a single, worldwide organization headed by a pope or world synod
of bishops or at least held together by a more or less tightly knit
structure. They contend that this type of unity satisfies Christ's prayer
that all be one better than the more nebulous concept of a spiritual
unity. To speak only of spiritual unity is to hold a docetic view
of the church. The church is not just a spiritual entity; it is a
continuation of the incarnation. Thence its unity requires tangible
and visible expression. Such visible unity allows the best opportunity
for witness to the church's one Lord.

The difficulty with this view is a practical one: Is such a worldwide
organizational unity possible or even feasible? None that incorporated
all Christians has ever existed—neither in the earliest period of
Christian history nor in the era after Constantine nor in the Middle
Ages nor in the Reformation and post-Reformation eras. Indeed,
efforts to secure such visible unity have failed repeatedly, often
entailing coercion and bloodshed, which always repel rather than
attract persons. To a large degree the growth of rationalism and
secularism in the era of the Enlightenment and after was a product
of the revulsion many developed in reaction to religious persecution
and warfare. The price of such unity, therefore, is much too high
and, what is worse, counterproductive. Presently Roman Catholics
are discovering that any unity must take the pluralism of humanity
fully into account.

The remaining option would seem, therefore, to lie somewhere
between the two extremes. Perhaps this could be framed in terms
of seeking natural ways to express visible unity without pursuit of
a grand scheme for the reunion of all Christians into one structure.
In light of history many groups, such as Baptists, have long feared
binding commitments that inhibit the freedom of individuals and
local congregations. Sentiments of this kind have developed with
the growth of individual consciousness in western society since the
Renaissance. Today they are heard as frequently among Roman

Catholics as among Baptists, and we can only expect further development. Consequently, this concern must be taken fully into account in unitive efforts, lest the latter cause greater damage, as they often have. Indeed, a few mergers that have not caused further rifts can be documented. Better the present array than a host of new sects or denominations.

Ecumenical Possibilities

Ecumenical propects would appear to be more viable in the direction of dialogue, cooperation, and communion than in the direction of union or merger. At the grass-roots level the feeling of oneness among Christians is strong, but it does not lend itself to support of ecumenical structures. Rather, as Ross MacKenzie [2] has pointed out, denominational consciousness in America is shifting as a result of years of moving from one denomination to another. Within every local congregation one may discern an ecumenical hodgepodge.

For example, a Baptist church would consist of persons of essentially Methodist, Presbyterian, Episcopal, Disciples', or even Roman Catholic as well as Baptist perceptions. Even if most members were Baptist, therefore, they would have developed a high level of tolerance for persons from other backgrounds and would have lowered their defensiveness about Baptist views. In many cases they have actually opted for views and practices of other traditions as being preferable to traditional Baptist ones. The worship of a certain Baptist congregation, for instance, may not differ noticeably from that of an Episcopal congregation, on one extreme, or a Quaker congregation, on the other.

The motive for union of churches is probably weakened as much as strengthened by this mixture. Many persons at any rate simply do not see the need for structural realignments. Why seek more visible expression of a tangible unity? Better to leave a good thing alone. The Consultation on Church Union, an exciting merger effort involving diverse denominations, floundered and died. Perhaps it was a dream that inspired too few persons to succeed. At the grass roots people are content with the unity they experience already.

Dialogue. One genuinely viable mode of expressing Christian unity is dialogue. Dialogues are going on at all levels among the major

Christian traditions—Roman Catholic, Orthodox, Protestant, Anglican—and even beyond. In some instances, these dialogues are looking toward merger or at least intercommunion. Anglican and Roman Catholic theologians, for example, have reached agreement on several items that could lead in a short time to a restoration of their communion. Some Orthodox churches have already agreed on intercommunion. Lutheran and Roman Catholic theologians have explored numerous thorny issues that divide them, including the primacy of the bishop of Rome.

In most instances, the dialogues involve chiefly an effort to achieve better understanding of those things that divide or unite us. Most persons, of course, enter this venture apprehensively, fearful that they may lose their own identity. Surprisingly, the opposite often happens. Discussion and exchange of views tends to sharpen one's denominational identity and to enhance appreciation for his or her own heritage as well as that for the heritage of others. Moreover, Christians who engage in dialogue deepen their understanding and appreciation for their common faith and heritage.

Cooperation. Dialogue frequently leads to cooperative efforts. Doing things together is and has been surely the *most* authentic expression of Christian unity. Specific ways in which this cooperation occurs will be discussed in a later chapter. It will suffice here to underline its importance in an age of world crisis. As a matter of fact, the ecumenical movement has shifted its main thrust from Christians and their unity to the world and its needs. At Uppsala in 1968 the assembly of the World Council of Churches repeatedly asserted that "the world writes the agenda for the Church" and, quoting Dietrich Bonhoeffer, called for the churches to be, like Jesus, "the Man for others." If many have welcomed a withdrawal from this position to a more traditional stance, it would be unfortunate to see a complete retreat at a time when the survival of humankind may depend on the joint effort of all persons of goodwill. The ecumenical efforts have frequently stumbled. Sometimes one denomination might have done a better job. But the overall record of the sixties and seventies has been impressive.

Communion. No symbol speaks more impressively about the unity of Christians than the Lord's Supper or Eucharist. The apostle Paul perceived it as *the* symbol of unity par excellence. It was a rebuke to the factions of the Corinthian church, for it epitomizes the self-giving love of Christ himself, which brings the church into existence. It symbolizes the covenant we have made with God in Christ and with one another (1 Cor. 11:17 ff.). At the same time no Christian observance has divided Christians more than this one, precisely because it is the chief symbol of communion. In the Reformation, even interpretation of the Supper divided Catholics from Protestants and Protestants from Protestants.

At the moment the question is: Should the Lord's Supper stand as a symbol of Christian division or of Christian unity? Some would make it the former. They offer communion only to persons of like faith and order on the grounds that communion should express actual formal unity based on participation in the same church body. To refuse communion to persons of other denominations is intended to point up the divided state of the church. In reality, it does more than this. What it suggests is that the group withholding communion in this way is the paradigm of Christianity. Indeed, some who practice closed communion, such as Landmark Baptists, make no effort to disguise such a claim. They and they alone represent authentic Christianity; others are poor imitations.

Others (and I am one) would make the Lord's Supper a symbol of the unity that Christ gives the church. This would mean admitting all who confess faith in God through Christ, regardless of other elements of faith and order, even of beliefs about the Lord's Supper itself. The fact is, denominational affiliation today has little to do with either faith or order. Each denomination, especially populous ones, represents the whole spectrum of both. Hence it seems wise to require only the test Paul proposed: "Let each person so examine himself (or herself) and then let him (her) eat" (1 Cor. 11:28). In this way responsibility for disunity would rest on those persons who refused communion and not on the church. Although it might tend also to level out denominations, it would eliminate false claims of finality by any group.

Ecumenical Organizations. Expressions of unity such as those discussed above will not lessen the importance of ecumenical organizations, whether local, national, or the World Council of Churches.

It is evident, to be sure, that the interest these organizations once generated has shifted. In the United States the National Council of Churches has tried to respond to this by developing a looser organization. The World Council, however, confronts such vast changes that restructuring may not solve the problem. What would happen, for instance, if the Roman Catholic Church applied for formal membership, since Roman Catholics outnumber all other Christians put together? What will happen as "third world" churches, which are growing at an amazing rate, begin to outnumber European and North American churches? What is now to be done with growing nationalism reflected in the assemblies that meet every seven years? Against this background the purpose of the World Council is growing more and more uncertain. Is it a world forum where Christians can discuss their efforts? Is it a means of sharing fellowship and information? Is it an organization designed to promote mergers or cooperative efforts? Older definitions of purpose no longer suffice. The ecumenical picture is unclear. Nevertheless, all Christians should be working through the existent organizations toward a clarification of it.

Relationships with Non-Christians

If the ecumenical picture is uncertain, what depicts Christian relationships with persons of other religious faiths is even more unclear. Until recently, this was an issue posed chiefly for missionary purposes. How do we approach people in foreign lands who belong to other faiths? Recently, however, the issue has been raised for Christians living in America by an influx of Oriental religions or religious practices that have proven attractive to many persons. Transcendental Meditation, for example, while disclaiming the label of a religion, has attracted millions of students across the land on account of its practical values.

Throughout many centuries Christians gave a single answer to the question of Christianity's relationships to the religions of mankind, whether primitive or advanced: Christianity is the one religion that can claim finality. The development of modern critical methodology in the nineteenth century, however, began to introduce some skepticism about this claim. For one thing, objective study of the religions showed a cross fertilization. Some scholars went so far as to argue that Christianity was itself an Oriental mystery religion founded by Paul rather than Jesus, whose existence they doubted. They pointed out that such religions borrowed from one another and from other sources willy-nilly. For another thing, comparative study of Christianity and other modern faiths revealed similarity on many points. This was most obvious in the case of Christianity's ancestor, Judaism, but it was evident also in other instances. On both counts, Christianity's claims to uniqueness were shattered. Meantime, a more dynamic conception of history appeared out of the influence of Darwin's theory of evolution and studies of primitive religions.

The nineteenth-century response to all of these developments was to argue an evolution of religion from the primitive state to Christianity. Like humanity, religion too evolved. Christianity was not *the* religion but the *highest* of the religions. Its evolution began with the early tribal religion of the Hebrews, in which Yahweh was God of the tribe. It reached a new level in the monotheistic legislation of Moses, which had to be purified by the prophets. Finally, it reached its peak in Jesus' proclamation of the gospel, which meant liberation from Mosaic legalism.

This attitude held sway for a long time in liberal circles, although it never captured the conservative mind. Its hold was broken, however, in 1918, with the dramatic entrance of Karl Barth's commentary on Romans, in which he argued for the uniqueness of Christianity on the basis of revelation. Christianity was not one among the many; it was not even a religion. Rather, it was life itself revealed by God in Jesus Christ. There can be no saving revelation apart from him. In 1937 Hendrik Kraemer developed Barth's views more fully with reference to the world's religions, contending strongly for its uniqueness and thus laying a firm foundation for the Christian mission.

In recent years the neoorthodox theology of Barth and Kraemer has fallen on hard times. Once again, many questions have been raised about Christian claims to uniqueness and finality. The prevailing posture toward other religions is expressed in the word *dialogue*. Except among conservatives, efforts to win converts from among the adherents of other religions are criticized. Indeed, the world missionary enterprise suffers from confusion and even failure of nerve.

Combined with growing nationalism, the lack of nerve is changing the approach of many Christian groups dramatically. Christianity's relationship to the other religions, therefore, is a pressing one. It needs serious consideration.

Judaism

Special consideration must be given to Judaism for several reasons. One is the fact that Judaism is Christianity's parent religion. One cannot understand Christianity apart from Judaism, especially as regards their common heritage in the Old Testament. Another is the fact that both Judaism and Christianity are monotheistic. Jews and Christians worship the same universal God, the Father of Abraham, Isaac, Jacob, and Jesus of Nazareth. This means that we are bound together not only by history but by faith.

A third is the experience of the Jews at the hands of Christians or supposedly Christian nations. The story of harassment and persecution of Jews by Christians is, of course, not a new one; it goes back to the fourth century of the Christian era. But his story had a chapter added to it which marked the *end* of one epoch of Jewish history and the beginning of another. I refer to the Holocaust, the massacre of six million Jews by Hitler and his demonic followers. Never again will Jewish people be able to relate to Christians as they have in the past. For them the Nazi pogrom marked the beginning of a new age and supplied the final impetus for the founding of a Jewish state. It also increased the number of skeptics and atheists of Jewish background.

Against the background of the Holocaust, how should Christians relate to the Jewish people?

First, the experience of the Holocaust, which boggles the mind for its horror, should awaken a new sensitivity to Jewish feelings toward Christians. For centuries Jewish people have lived in fear of Christian reprisal. This is evident even in America, where the Constitution has guaranteed religious freedom; legal sanctions can never eliminate prejudice and acts of hatred. Anti-Semitism rears its ugly head often enough to keep Jewish people vigilant. It is not inconceivable that, even in the United States, subtle prejudices could fan sparks into a flame.

This suggests, secondly, that Christians need seriously to examine the roots of anti-Semitism, particularly as they are exposed in the New Testament. Christian anti-Semitism is rooted in the conviction that the Jews put Jesus to death. Stated without qualification, as it usually has been since New Testament times, this charge is false. *Some* Jews, notably the ruling circle, undoubtedly did play a role in Jesus' execution; but not *all* Jews did so. Jesus had many admirers and followers among his people. Indeed, the church began *within* Judaism, consisting of Jews only. To be precise, the Romans, not the Jews, put Jesus to death for rather vague reasons but probably on a charge of insurrection. If certain Jewish leaders played a role, it was that of accomplices.

To develop greater sensitivity to Jewish people and to grapple with the problem of anti-Semitism, thirdly, some Christians are engaging in dialogue with Jews. Conservative Christians may find this a bit frightening, but it is equally so for Jewish people, who are in the minority everywhere in the world. Moreover, dialogue holds immense benefits. It raises the level of appreciation and, surprisingly, reinforces faith on both sides while breaking down prejudices. Jews, of course, like Christians, have varied religious views. They fall roughly into four groups: (1) Orthodox, (2) Conservative, (3) Reformed, and (4) secular. They are also highly individualistic, and, if nothing else, dialogue will help Christians to discern the pluralism of Judaism and to get to know some persons as individuals. In the final analysis, the latter effort will bring the greatest reward.

There remains, however, the question of *witness* to Jewish people about Christ. Against the background of the Holocaust this is a highly sensitive matter, for the Christian conviction about the finality of Christ has fostered and fueled anti-Semitism and persecution. Some persons would repudiate any witness being directed to Jewish people. Others, on the other hand, would continue very much along traditional lines, exerting every effort to win some. I would steer between the two extremes. Witness, by any religious group, is always permissible and appropriate. In its proper sense it manifests our personal concern for others. The crucial issue, therefore, is not *whether* but *how* we witness. To consider the matter with the shoe on the other foot, I would not object if a Jewish person witnessed to me about his or her faith in God. I *would* object to application of psychological or other pressures to force me to adopt Judaism and to belittling of Christianity at the expense of Judaism. Only a little recollection will remind us that Christians have frequently erred in using questionable means to win converts. We Christians should have the same respect for Jews, or persons of any other faith, as we would expect from them.

Other Faiths

Other religions will not hold the same place as Judaism in Christian eyes, but all merit a more positive appreciation than Christians have usually granted them. There may even be a special niche for Islam alongside Judaism by virtue of the fact that it too is monotheistic and an heir of both Judaism and Christianity. The issue that should be raised for all the others, however, is the extent to which Christians can learn from them and have something to contribute to them.

At one time Christians of the West looked with condescension upon eastern religions in light of a negative judgment rendered upon the cultures they produced. A Christian civilization, it was argued, produced science and technology. These helped foster a superior culture, raising the level of human life markedly. Contrariwise, Oriental religions retarded the development of science and technology and thus of Oriental culture. These cultures, consequently, have not aided the achievement of human potential as the Christian-influenced western culture has.

Recently crises that are largely outgrowths of the application of science and technology—wars, overconsumption, waste, ecological imbalance—have caused us to reexamine this prideful attitude. Astute observers such as Thomas Merton have been asking whether the West does not need to learn from Oriental wisdom. Have Christians of the West perhaps lost some of the insights inherent in their once Oriental faith? Could they learn something from Oriental religions that might help them to use natural resources and even the products of their technology more wisely? Could they learn, for instance, how to seek wisdom for its own sake, truth, the ground of being, God? The fact is, Christianity has created something that leads to increasing secularity. Ultimately, God and religion may be edged out entirely.

Undoubtedly, Christians can learn much from other faiths and thus should welcome the current trend toward dialogue. As in dialogue with persons of Jewish faith, such encounters can foster mutual understanding and appreciation and deepen appreciation for one's own faith.

There arises again, of course, the question of witness. Once more, both Christians and persons of other faiths should feel free to witness to others. It is true that other religions may have less motivation for this witness than the monotheistic religions—Judaism, Christianity, and Islam—but all religions have considerable interest in self-propagation. As a matter of fact, several of the Oriental religions are experiencing a resurgence of missionary fervor and making a substantial impact in the West. Problems arise here, as I noted earlier, not from witness but from certain ways of witnessing. Every effort should be made by all religions to respect the convictions of persons of other faiths sufficiently that personal integrity will not be violated. In the present day dialogue may represent the best type of witness to persons of other faiths.

Common Enemy and Common Effort

Before closing this discussion of Christianity's relationship to other religions, a word should be added concerning the common enemy all religions face and the possibility of mutual effort. The common enemy is the increase of godlessness, dehumanization, depersonalization, and numerous by-products of these. I have already quoted Arnold Toynbee's graphic warning that humanity faces the greatest peril to its survival it has faced since the beginning of human existence. The source of this problem, and also its solution, lies not in technology and science per se but in human use. Since the seventeenth century, westerners have proceeded apace in the development of an industrial, a superindustrial, and now a postindustrial civilization. In moral and spiritual progress, however, they have not stayed abreast of their technological advance. Until the former catches up with the latter, the crises will become more and more severe.

At least part of the solution lies in the hands of the world's religions. They alone can help us to rediscover the "rock from whence we were hewn." Conservative persons in all of these faiths will concede only with great reservations that the other faiths may contribute something too. To admit that, however, is not to deny the truth of one's own faith. For a Christian to learn from a Buddhist how to meditate, for example, is not to belittle what Christianity promises.

I am not arguing for a hodgepodge religion. The truth of the matter is, each religion is a self-contained unit. It can only be understood in the cultural package and history in which it came. No one could amalgamate the insights of the world's religions. They go with the package. What will emerge from dialogue and mutual effort, rather, will be deeper perceptions of our own faith and perhaps rediscovery of insights badly needed in our day.

Part III
The Mission
of the Church

7
Structuring for Mission

The title of this chapter suggests a particular perspective about the church's institutions and programs. Whereas many theologians would discuss structures under the nature of the church, I have deferred such discussion to the beginning of a consideration of the church's mission. In doing so, I am suggesting that structures are related more intimately to what the church does than to what it is and that they belong to its essence chiefly insofar as the church is in essence mission. Stated another way, the church must have institutions and programs in order to discharge its mission; but it is debatable whether it has to have *particular* institutions and programs. The latter are adaptable and expendable according to the extent to which they assist the churches in achieving their mission.

Institutions and Identity

Before proceeding with our discussion of the way the church structures for mission, however, I must enter a qualifying statement about institutions and programs in relation to the church's identity. Particular institutions or practices help to establish the identity of the church inasmuch as they provide continuity with the past. Without certain tangible forms and structures of its own that anchored it to the past, the church would open itself unguardedly to the caprice of contemporary cultures. In our own day, for example, the business model exercises a pervasive influence. In that fact itself there is no serious problem. But there is a problem if the influence of the model dominates to such an extent that it perverts or corrupts certain values that are fundamental to the Christian faith and life.

Consider for a moment the operation of one urban church. The corporation (congregation) elects a board (deacons), which sets the goals for the corporation (w number of conversions or additions, x number of new buildings, y income in tithes and offerings, z amount of satisfaction among stockholders). The board hires an executive (pastor), offering salary and benefits competitive with those offered by other churches. It outlines for him the expectations of the corporation. If the executive fails to meet the goals, the board sets a time within which he can be expected to improve his performance. If he cannot meet the goals, he will be replaced; and a new and more competent executive will be secured.

Under pressure to meet the demands, the executive applies proven sales and consumer methods. He advertises that Jesus will meet every need—physical or spiritual. He puts on a "show" every Sunday. He gives away bicycles and TVs for attendance prizes by groups. He buses people from the larger metropolitan area and beyond. Bus drivers win prizes for the largest loads. To attract as many persons as possible, they give away candy bars and balloons and hide five-dollar bills under certain seats. Thus the corporation blossoms and grows!

The issue here is: How do we evaluate the propriety of this obviously exaggerated influence of the business model? What is to be the safeguard against its subversion of essential truths of the church?

The answer to these questions rests in great part in the tested forms and structures that the church has conserved from the beginning on. Admittedly, Christians do not agree as to which forms and structures these are. On one extreme, Quakers have in theory rejected all forms except the voluntary assembling of believers. They do not observe any sacraments but regard all things as sacramental. In practice most Quakers have employed Scriptures as an authority and developed a more or less formal ministry—a confirmation, I think, of the need of some forms for the sake of identity.

On the other extreme, Roman Catholics, at least until the Second Vatican Council, have relied on an essentially institutional model for the church and thus identified it by numerous forms and structures: seven sacraments, Scriptures, decisions of twenty-one ecumenical councils, the hierarchy, and, especially, the papacy as the supreme teaching authority.

Somewhere in between these extremes, Orthodox Christians and Anglicans have attached Christian identity to two sacraments, the decisions of the first seven (or four for Anglicans) ecumenical councils, and episcopal succession. Most mainline Protestants, including Baptists, have followed Luther and Calvin in defining the church according to "where the Word is rightly preached and the sacraments are properly administered." Radical Protestants such as Mennonites have identified the church much more decisively in terms of church discipline, enjoined by the Scriptures; but they also have observed baptism, Lord's Supper, and even footwashing. They have an ordered ministry.

Where one strikes the spectrum today will doubtless depend to a large degree on the tradition to which he or she belongs. Speaking from the perspective of the Baptist tradition and as a church historian, I would single out the following forms and structures as essential not only for effecting the church's mission but for conserving its identity as a missionary people in the context of pervasive cultural influence.

Record of Witness to Divine Self-disclosure

The first and most essential of these would be the record of testimonies to God's self-disclosure in history. Christianity, like Judaism, is based upon a conviction that God has disclosed himself and his purposes for humanity in certain historical events. What we can know or recall of this disclosure has been conserved in the writings of the Old and New Testaments. These contain the record of those who bore witness to certain revelatory events, the mighty acts of God that began with Abraham and reached their fullness in Jesus of Nazareth. While later generations can conserve and retell the story of these events, they cannot reproduce the events themselves. Their witness, therefore, is always secondary, dependent on the testimony of those who were, as Luke stated it, "eye witnesses . . . of the word" (Luke 1:2).

The point is especially crucial in the case of the Christ-event, for it is a fundamental tenet of Christian faith that the divine self-disclosure reached its final and definitive expression in Jesus of Nazareth. Whereas in the Old Testament era God spoke in a partial and piecemeal fashion in the prophets, in this event he spoke his definitive word "in his Son . . . heir of all things, through whom he made the world, . . . the effulgence of his own weighty presence and express image of his own person" (Heb. 1:2; author's paraphrase). In John's words, "the Word became flesh and dwelt among us" (John 1:14).

Although one or two tidbits about Jesus have survived apart from the writings now found in our New Testament canon, we are dependent almost entirely upon the latter for what firsthand evidence we can have of this crucial event. It is not surprising that early Christians elected certain of these documents for reading in public worship and instruction along with the Old Testament canon used in Judaism. Without these, Christian memory of the Christ-event would have become increasingly vague and inexact and eventually distorted.

Guides to Interpretation

A moment's reflection will point up at this juncture the need for a second form, for a guide to the interpretation of these testimonies. It is true that the essential message of the Scriptures is relatively clear and can be understood by most persons when translated into the vernacular. The very fact that translation is required, however, shows that experts enter into the process somewhere and that interpretation is not as simple as some suppose. To the contrary, it is an exceedingly complicated task, requiring first the establishment of a proper text, then interpretation of words in context, consideration of literary forms, and many other factors. It is easy enough to see why, in the process of interpreting, some run aground on obscure passages whose context is difficult to ascertain and read into the Scriptures what they wish to find there. Thus distortion, sometimes severe distortion, occurs. The risk requires some safeguards vis-à-vis interpretation. In the history of the church three have normally been applied.

1. One is the rule of *interpreting Scriptures* (especially those that are obscure) *by Scriptures* (that are clear). The Protestant reformers, Calvin in particular, made much of this rule as they repudiated both creed and ecclesiastical teaching authority. The values of the method

are evident, but it did not eliminate the problem of contorted or erroneous interpretation. The reformers soon returned to confessional statements that could guide interpretation. By the second generation a Protestant scholasticism replaced the scholasticism of the medieval church. Words of the reformers themselves became the chief guides to interpretation. There was, in effect, not only a creed but a teaching office, one that could deal summarily with heresy and heretics such as Michael Servetus.

2. What this says is that other things besides the Scriptures themselves will inevitably enter the picture regarding their interpretation. The second, as the first Christians learned early, is the *confession of faith* made at baptism and sometimes used in instruction, worship, defense of the faith, and exorcism. There is always a risk of credalism in the employment of confessions, but no one may deny the necessity of confessions from the beginning. Embedded in the earliest New Testament writings, Paul's letters, are confessions of different types. The earliest probably contained one article—confession of faith in Christ (Rom. 10:9; Phil. 2:6-11; 1 Tim. 3:16). Next came two-part—of the Father and the Son (1 Cor. 8:6)—and three-part confessions—of Father, Son, and Spirit (Matt. 28:19-20). In essence, a confession of faith has both an affective and a cognitive side. It phrases symbolically the personal covenant that a believer makes with God. The confession lapses into credalism when the personal element is effaced by the cognitive or perhaps lost entirely.

Throughout history confessions have served more or less as summaries of the main tenets of faith and thus as guides to interpretation of the Scriptures. Since they were employed long before a New Testament canon came into existence, it is not correct to see them merely as summaries of the Scriptures. Actually they contain the earliest *oral* tradition used in instructing and baptizing converts from the beginning. In the life of the church, however, they underwent a process of growth and refinement in response to threats of heresy at different periods. Thus they are historically conditioned and should not be placed on the same level as the Scriptures as containing revelation, a fact which even Roman Catholics acknowledged in the Second Vatican Council.

Considered with proper regard for this historical conditioning, however, they can show us some of the elements that Christians have seen as the norms of faith and some of the pitfalls that they sought to avoid. To steer clear of credalism, it will be necessary to accentuate the secondary role of confessions and to subordinate them to the revelation contained in the Scriptures alone.

3. The third guide to the interpretation of the Scriptures that Christians have employed has been *a teaching office recognized by the church.* Protestants, of course, have long denied that they had a teaching office. In comparison with the closely structured Roman Catholic *magisterium*, which places the final decision in papal hands, such a denial would be accurate. In a broader sense, however, it is not, for, with the exception of the most individualistic Christian sects, every Christian group possesses some kind of teaching office that exercises influence or authority with respect to interpreting the Scriptures for the whole body.

Among Baptists, who are in many ways very individualistic, for example, each congregation exercises influence if not direct authority in interpretation. Beyond this level associations, state conventions, national conventions, and various boards and agencies exercise significant influence. Thus there is a teaching office, but it is decentralized. The important thing for a teaching office, as for confessions of faith, is that it too should be subordinated to the revelation contained in the Scriptures. Abuse of such authority, whether by individuals or corporate units, usually derives from claims of absoluteness that place the teaching office above rather than below the Word of God.

Given the level of individual consciousness that is experienced today, the effective operation of a teaching office depends on the trust that individuals and church groups place in their leaders. Power models will vary widely, but the dogmatic model of the past—for example, of the Middle Ages—is becoming less and less viable. As a matter of fact, most denominations now find themselves caught in a crisis of authority. Models that might be viable in the future have not emerged yet, but it is clear that they will have to take fuller account of popular opinion, perhaps by a sort of plebiscite, and strive for some kind of consensus.

To do so, of course, creates a tension between the desire of experts to be faithful to revelation and what people will accept, between what is right and what is possible. During the fifties and sixties, for example, the interpreters of the Scriptures could say, "Segregation of blacks and whites is contrary to the Scriptures. Oneness of all persons is the goal set by revelation." To eliminate segregation and to effect this unity, however, was another matter, one which has yet to be resolved. One of the results of the growth of individual consciousness is that it has increased not only the freedom but the tendency of individual Christians to decide issues such as this one for themselves. In many ways this is an asset, for it means that individuals may assume more responsibility for their actions. In other ways it is a liability, for it means that they may choose to disregard the teachings of Scriptures or those who interpret them, as in the case of segregation.

After considerable study of the authority crisis in both Roman Catholic and Protestant churches, I would conclude that the severe challenge of the moment may inspire all of the churches to do a better job of teaching. The aim of instruction should be the inculcation not of fixed ideas but of individual responsibility. As long as individual consciousness continues to increase, the churches' leaders will have to be satisfied with the present questioning of authority and seek to convince in both head and heart that the truths with which they have been entrusted are worth believing and applying.

Symbols of a Common Life

Besides the Scriptures and certain guides to interpretation, the church's identity also depends on common activities and symbols. A common worship surely is essential, belonging to the church's essence. Whether *common* means "uniform," however, has long been mooted. The Roman, Orthodox, and Anglican churches, on the one hand, have opted for standardized liturgies.

Most Protestants, on the other hand, have insisted on a limited number of fixed elements in their liturgies. Indeed, radical Protestants have eschewed the use of the word *liturgy* as significative of a formality and a fixity that they oppose in worship. From their earliest days in seventeenth-century England, for example, Baptists have not been able to lay aside an aversion to standardized worship, sometimes going to ridiculous extremes in spontaneity. This attitude, however, has spread beyond descendants of the radical reformers. Since the Second Vatican Council many Roman Catholics have joined the throng of Protestants favoring spontaneity over formality.

The future does not look bright for uniformity in worship, therefore. We must have common worship, but we do not have to have one liturgy applicable to all. How this worship may vitalize the church will be discussed later. Presently we shall look at the contribution two symbols make to the church's identity.

Baptism and Lord's Supper or Eucharist are symbols which Christians have employed through the centuries and which supply continuity with Christians of all ages. Some persons, however, are skeptical of the continuing value of observing these rites, especially baptism. In the Bampton Lectures for 1968 F. W. Dillistone[1] argued that, to be viable, symbols must strike a deep chord in the experience of the people who observe them. While he thought the observance of the Lord's Supper still does that, he doubted whether baptism does. Another factor, however, determines the significance of symbols in Christianity—historical experience.

Jesus himself and his earliest followers poured meaning into observances that would otherwise have had little meaning. They made baptism and Lord's Supper convenant ceremonies bound up with the life, death, and resurrection of Jesus. In baptism a new convert acted out in a parabolic form his or her participation with Jesus in the servant's role. In Paul's words, he or she died and rose with Christ (Rom. 6:4). In the Lord's Supper a Christian continually renewed the pledge made at baptism. While it is true, then, that baptism or Lord's Supper may not carry as much obvious significance for persons who live in modern technological societies as they had for the first Christians, it would be a mistake to substitute more modern ones. These two symbols are history-laden, their meaning determined in great part by connection with a specific historical event. They probably get less meaning from the present than from the past. To lay them aside altogether would be to forfeit their value as symbols of Christianity's integral connection with the Christ-event.

This is not to say that all Christians must adopt a single mode of observance and interpretation of these symbols. Not even the creed has occasioned more fierce debate than interpretation and observance of baptism and Lord's Supper. Today the debate is less passionate and, by a return to the Scriptures and history, more tolerant of diversity, for a study of these rites in history shows ample room for variety of opinion.

Structures and Mission

Some Christians would add a set form of ministry to the items I have associated with the identity of the church. Roman Catholics, Anglicans, and Orthodox, for example, insist on apostolic succession through ordination of bishops as a guarantee of the Church's faith and ministry. Based on a study of history, however, the church must have an ordered ministry; but that ministry does not have to assume a particular form. Rather, it can be adapted so as to meet the needs of the Christian mission. It is precisely this ·that occurred in early Christian history.

Early Christianity spread chiefly through the planting of churches. The apostle Paul, who set the style for the mission, established churches in cities that were centers of commerce and culture in as many Roman provinces as possible. The structures of the early churches varied. The Jerusalem church had something like an episcopal structure headed by James, the brother of Jesus. Corinth had a more congregational structure with no definite offices (1 Cor. 12:28). Most churches probably assumed an organization similar to that of the Jewish synagogue, with presbyters or elders and deacons.

In time the third form prevailed. In each city presbyters, also called bishops, functioned as a board. They assumed responsibility for the mission of the church in the whole city and even beyond. Little by little, Christianity spread outward from the cities to the surrounding countryside.

Late in the first century or early in the second a change in the structures of most churches began to occur. It was prompted in part by threats of heresy but also in part by the needs of a growing church. The presiding presbyter began to acquire greater authority. The term bishop was reserved for him alone. Thus emerged a threefold structure for each city: bishop, presbyters, and deacons.

Ordination by laying on of hands, of course, developed early as a symbolic way of attesting those whose gifts the churches recognized.

To what extent it connoted the handing on of apostolic authority is a matter of heated debate, not to be resolved here. There can be no question that the practice was soon interpreted in that way as threats of heresy reared up. By the late second century Irenaeus, Bishop of Lyons, formulated the classic position, citing lists of bishops going back to the apostles who could guarantee doctrine. To be sure of orthodoxy, all churches needed to formulate their doctrine in such a way as to *agree* with the doctrine of these churches. The specific list that Irenaeus happened to cite was that of Roman bishops, but it is quite clear from his statement that he knew others and regarded them too as valid norms for doctrine. The fact that he cited the Roman list, however, has been used to support a theory of Roman primacy and authority that Irenaeus would not have accepted.

That the early churches soon recognized ordination as a means of safeguarding the church against heresy in no way negates the point being made here, that structures remained adaptable to the demands of the mission. Even after Constantine, church structures continued to develop. Immediately after Constantine's conversion church organization proliferated as the churches, no longer persecuted, sought to establish a Christian witness in every nook and cranny of the Roman Empire.

When overlap occasioned by expansion of churches from cities to the surrounding countryside caused jurisdictional disputes, church leaders decided to organize the churches along territorial lines. Accordingly, they adopted the political divisions of the Roman Empire, called dioceses, as church units. Later dioceses were divided into parishes. Within the diocese the bishop was the axle around which the work of the churches revolved. Serving with him, however, were numerous others: presbyters, deacons, subdeacons, janitors, doorkeepers, deaconesses, exorcists, and many others.

It is often overlooked that the overarching pattern of early Christianity had missionary implications. From a very early date the mission was conceived of under the ideology of the "Army of Christ" (*Militia Christi*) engaged in battle with the forces of evil (Eph. 6:10-20). Baptism was the lay person's ordination. In it the new convert pledged allegiance to Christ and prepared to fight Satan and his hosts. Laying on of hands set some apart for leadership roles in the missionary people of God. The ordained were those commissioned with special responsibility in recognition of their gifts, but all were to pursue the mission together.

The military motif may not commend itself to many persons today. But what all of this suggests to me is that, while retaining stability around ordination, the church may adapt and accommodate its structures and programs to discharge its mission. An official ministry, by whatever titles it may be designated, will always be necessary. Its purpose is to coordinate the total effort of the people of God. At the same time nothing should stand in the way of churches developing whatever ecclesial or para-ecclesial ministries the discharge of their mission requires.

Whom Do We Ordain?

Some new types of ministry being developed will be discussed in a later chapter. Presently, it will be useful to examine more closely the range of ordination, for the proliferation of specialties and also the issue of women's rights have raised serious questions about the current practice in most denominations. The New Testament does not contain much data about ordination. In the four instances where laying on of hands refers to ordination (Acts 6:6; 13:3; 1 Tim. 4:14; 2 Tim. 1:6) the context has to do with the setting apart of certain persons for leadership roles in the Christian mission. In each case the laying on of hands symbolized an earlier sign from God, discernible by others, of certain gifts for these roles. Indeed, according to Acts 13:1-3 and 1 Timothy 4:14, prophets were consulted to determine the authenticity of the gifts.

These passages suggest two criteria we might use to determine whom we should ordain: (1) whether someone plays a *leading* role, not just any role, in the fulfillment of the church's mission, and (2) whether someone shows gifts that are discernible by others. These criteria address directly the problems of both proliferation of ministries and ordination of women. They might also discourage the rash of hasty ordinations that later lead to abandonment of certain church-related roles with considerable feelings of guilt.

The proliferation problem. The problem of proliferation of ministries arises largely out of change from an agrarian to an urban society. When America was largely rural, most congregations, being small, required only one minister to meet their needs. As America has become predominately urban, however, the variety of required ministries has expanded for several reasons.

For one thing, congregations have grown larger and more diverse. Those with memberships in the thousands cannot be adequately served by a single minister; they require multiple ministries. The more ministers there are, the greater the possibility of specialization. For another, urban life makes greater demands on people and supplies more specialized aids. Whereas general theological training of a single minister once sufficed in rural areas, it will not suffice today. Large churches that have resources to meet diverse needs with specially trained personnel stand a better chance of attracting and assisting members than small ones. They meet urban society on its own terms when they employ specialists in education, music, counseling, social service, legal aid, and other areas. For a third, in the fifties and sixties the churches of America became more involved in society and its needs. Whereas before they envisioned mission largely in terms of gathering, now they envision it in terms of scattering and becoming involved.

What has happened to individual congregations has happened also to denominations. To meet the requirements of the churches they serve, denominational boards, agencies, and the like have increased their special services. The result is that they employ persons of widely diversified skills—ranging from executives to printers, from teachers to recreation directors, and from program designers to cooks.

Who, then, should receive ordination? The number of persons requesting ordination has skyrocketed not only because of the clerical calling but also because of the tax exemptions it helps one obtain. The tax exemption issue is not a simple or an unimportant one, but the churches cannot settle the issue on such pragmatic grounds. Rather, they must decide on the basis of what ordination really signifies. If it signifies (1) leadership and (2) genuine calling, then the field has been narrowed considerably. These stipulations would avert the problem of the older rule—that is, a calling to pastoral ministry.

Obviously today many persons, both in local churches and else-where, fulfill genuine leadership roles not directly pastoral. These would merit ordination according to the rule I have drawn but not according to the older one. At the same time the new rule would eliminate hundreds of functions that did not qualify as leadership functions or as leading vocations. Local congregations, for instance, might legitimately ordain a pastor, an associate pastor, a minister of education, a minister of music, and a minister of youth on the grounds that each of these fulfilled leadership roles, but exclude paid staff members such as secretaries, counselors, teachers of nursery schools, and others.

The ordination of women. The issue of women's ordination vexes many denominations. It is made particularly thorny by the fact that New Testament writings leave evidence only for the ordination of women as deacons or deaconesses (Rom. 16:1; 1 Tim. 3:11) and contain certain statements that restrict the roles of women in the church. In 1 Corinthians 14:34-35, for example, Paul forbade women to speak in public assemblies (*ekklesiai*). Similarly, in 1 Timothy 2:12 he ruled that a woman could not teach or rule over her husband but was to learn in silence. Opponents of women's ordination, more-over, point out also that none of the twelve was a woman, even though Jesus had women among his followers and even through the centuries the churches did not ordain women to the offices of pres-byter or bishop.

Over against this evidence, however, stands a fundamental princi-ple of Christianity: "There is neither Jew nor Greek, there is neither slave nor free, there is neither male nor female; for you are all one in Christ Jesus" (Gal. 3:28). In this context it is clear that being "in Christ Jesus" means "in the church, the Body of Christ" (3:26-27). God's love (agape) does not take away natural differences, but it transcends them in such a way that we are united in one and become equal within Christ's body (1 Cor. 12). This means potentially that any Christian of proper qualifications—Jew, Gentile, freeborn, slave, male, or female—could hold any office.

How are we to resolve these conflicting attitudes? The answer surely resides in distinguishing between a principle—that there is no distinction in the church—and accommodation to a particular social situation. To cite a parallel situation, Paul stated that "there is neither slave nor free person" in Christ; but he insisted, too, on account of social context, that slaves remain as they were, bound to their masters (1 Cor. 7:21). It was not that Paul contradicted himself in supporting slavery as an institution; rather, it was a question of adapting to an unchangeable situation until the principle could be fully applied, as it eventually was.

Can we not draw an inference from this vis-à-vis the ordination of women? The principle would allow women to hold any office men held. Indeed, some women served alongside Paul in roles equivalent to those filled by men. Priscilla, for instance, was named *before* her husband half the times Luke and Paul referred to them (Acts 18:26; Rom. 16:3). But Paul did not push the application of the principle to its limit, for to do so would prove too disruptive socially, just as a campaign to emancipate slaves would have. Thus, excepting women prophets, he did not press for the rights of women to speak or teach, lest their doing so should disrupt both Jews and Gentiles too much.

The issue that must now be raised is whether we are far enough along socially, after centuries of Christian history, to apply the principle of equality more fully. Some denominations have. I believe western social perceptions would favor it. American society, for instance, is far down the road in assuring equal rights for women in numerous areas. Should the churches lag behind, or can they take a giant stride forward in recognizing in fact the roles women have long played?

Some Guidelines for Adapting Structures and Programs

Change is, as we noted earlier, not always beneficial. If we are to avoid caprice in adaptation of structures and programs of the church, we will need to follow certain guidelines for accommodation. I would recommend the following steps for congregational change:

1. *Study the nature and mission of the church.* To be effective, change requires a point of reference. Without that it will be capricious. A study of this sort can be done at various levels of church life, both local and regional.

2. *Survey the needs of the community.* For a local congregation

this can be done by way of a checklist such as that found in Gaines S. Dobbins' *Building Better Churches*.[2] The following represent major areas of study:

1. *Social conditions*
   a. Racial problems
   b. Community spirit
   c. Living conditions—housing, playgrounds, and so forth
   d. Delinquency
2. *Economic conditions*
   a. Wealth and poverty
   b. Unemployment
   c. Labor-management problems
   d. Use of resources
3. *Health conditions*
   a. Physical illness
   b. Mental illness, retardation
   c. Problems of santitation
4. *Family conditions*
   a. Marriage and family problems
   b. Institutions destructive of the family
5. *Educational conditions*
   a. Schools
   b. Cultural needs of various groups
   c. Backward and retarded children
6. *Recreational conditions*
   a. School facilities
   b. Public playgrounds and parks
   c. Commercial facilities
7. *Dependents*
   a. Care of orphans, deprived youth
   b. Aged
   c. Disabled

3. *State the objectives of the church in relationship to the particular situation.* In the sixties many critics assailed the essentially inward-looking orientation of the institutional churches and called for them to assume the role of servant to society. As wholesome and needed

as the latter was, however, it caused an imbalance. In responding, many churches neglected worship and education out of concern for ministry. The result was that they ended up trying to accomplish the tasks of a Charles Atlas with the physique of a ninety-five pound weakling. This cautions us, in formulating objectives, to be careful to strike a balance between being the church and doing what the church is to do. What some of the major objectives are will become clear in subsequent chapters.

4. *Develop plans and structures to achieve these objectives.* If, as I have argued, the church is not bound to particular programs or structures, then it is free to develop those that suit its particular situation. Often we will have to experiment with a variety of programs and structures. The chief limit will be the imagination and resources of groups of believers engaged in fulfilling particular objectives.

It will not be without value, however, to conclude this chapter by reminding ourselves that many of the programs and structures used in the past still have merit. Prayer, Bible study, corporate worship, personal concern, and many other things remain fundamental. They cannot be supplanted by gimmicks and slick programs. In the final analysis, the church's ministry is a very personal one. What it does cannot run counter to its essential nature as the people of God on mission in and to the world.

8
New Humanity and Mission

In the 1960s many, zealous to get the churches out of sheltered sanctuaries, accentuated mission as being in and to the world. The kingdom or rule of God is in the world, in the secular city, coming among persons there. It is not restricted to gatherings of the faithful and hallowed retreats.

This kind of thinking contained a wholesome and salutary emphasis even when it went to extremes. The wholesome aspect was the strong reminder that the church's mission is in and to the world and that the world should have some role in writing the church's agenda. There can be little doubt that Christianity is essentially a world-affirming faith. In the Christian view the world is God's creation. It is also the object of his redemptive activity, as John 3:16 makes clear. Even the fact that the world has fallen under sway of "the evil one" does not alter the divine concern for both the created order and the order human beings have imposed upon it.

The problem in this view lay in extremism—above all, in the assumption that, because mission is in and to the world, we do not need also to gather (to prepare, as it were) for mission. A study of the history of Christianity will demonstrate quickly that, when the churches have implemented the mission in and to the world most effectively, there has been persistence in education, fellowship, and worship. The latter should not be seen merely as *preparation* for mission but as an integral part of the mission itself. Each makes its own vital contribution to the building of the new humanity, the body of Christ; and in this process Christianity is effecting its chief goal, the unification of humanity and the universe. Not surprisingly, one of Christianity's most appealing points has been its fellowship, extended to all persons without regard for economic or social status, background, nationality, or any other qualification.

In an earlier chapter I discussed the nature of the new humanity. At this point we will examine more specifically how it is developed. Here Acts 2:42 supplies some instructive information about the building up of the new humanity.

In the last analysis, of course, the new humanity, the body of Christ, is God's creation. It does not depend on human effort. Just as God raised Christ from the dead, so also he, through his Spirit, creates and sustains his body, the church. At Pentecost, as Luke understood the beginning of the church, the Spirit poured out upon all and reversed Babel by uniting Parthians, Medes, Elamites, Mesopotamians, Judaeans, Cappadocians, and other persons of the ancient civilized world in fulfillment of Joel 2:28-29. The incident confirmed the experience of Jesus' resurrection, that death no longer held sway over him (Acts 2:24), and opened the possibility of others' sharing in the new life of the messianic era.

Thus the new humanity depends on God's action and not that of human beings. Nevertheless, it was also made clear by Luke that we too can do something to foster the experience of the new humanity. The Jerusalem community, he says, "were persisting in the teaching of the apostles and in fellowship, in the breaking of bread and in prayers" (Acts 2:42, author's translation). The key word here is the one I have translated "were persisting." The Greek word *proskartereo* is a strong one. In this context it suggests unrelenting devotion to these activities. As a result of such steadfastness, God used the community as a channel for effecting his purposes. There were numerous conversions. Charity abounded. Miracles occurred. A community had put itself at God's disposal, and he used it. Has there ever been another formula for mission that has been more effective? Conversely, has mission ever fallen into greater disrepair than when it neglected this formula?

Persistence in the Apostles' Teaching

At this juncture let us turn to examine the major elements of the Lucan formula for vitality in mission. The first of these is persistence in the apostles' teaching. *Persistence* is required because grasping the apostles' teaching and applying it to life are both simple and complex tasks.

On the one hand, they are *simple* in the sense that they involve a commitment of a personal nature, a surrender of heart and will to God, becoming as little children. In the last analysis, such a commitment does not require a sophisticated cerebral comprehension. It is the kind of decision that persons of limited intellectual comprehension, even children, can make. Indeed, the intellect, as believers through the centuries have pointed out, may get in the way of authentic commitment. It can create a casuistry that causes us to walk around the demands of this personal relationship rather than meeting it head on. The church's saints, in the stricter sense of the term, have often been persons whose hearts spoke more powerfully than their heads—persons like Francis of Assisi, Catherine of Siena, or John Woolman. They acted with a decisiveness and clarity of purpose that all of us are compelled to admire.

On the other hand, even considered in relational terms, the apostles' teaching is *complex*; to understand and to act on it requires persistence. However much we may consider it an affair of the heart, it is also an affair of the head. It has a cognitive as well as an affective side. As C. H. Dodd once summarized this teaching or preaching, it announces that the age of fulfillment has dawned.[1] This happened through the life, death, and resurrection of Jesus of Nazareth, which is confirmed by the outpouring of the Spirit upon all persons. He will return to consummate the event. The dawning of this age calls for repentance and faith as prerequisites for joining the community of the end time.

That it is not a simple matter to understand or to apply this teaching is confirmed by the struggle the first missionaries went through to clarify it for their converts. We may discern translation going on in all of the writings of the New Testament, but especially in Acts and Paul's letters. To the ears of persons of Greek background, this message sounded strange, incomprehensible, even nonsensical, until missionaries translated it into language they understood. Harbingers of the good news must often have received a reception like Paul's on Mars Hill in Athens: "He seems to be the herald of strange demons because he is preaching Jesus and resurrection . . . . Can we comprehend what this new teaching is which is spoken by you?

For you are introducing something foreign to our ears. We want, therefore, to know what these things are" (Acts 17:18-20, author's translation). It is not surprising, then, that, in order to win converts, Paul sought to "become all things to all [persons]" (1 Cor. 9:22).

As a matter of fact, his translation work is quite visible in his letters. He did much more than repeat a message he had received, although such a message obviously underlay all that he did (Gal. 1:6-9; 1 Cor. 15:3-8). He also undertook translation and application of it in idioms that converts of Gentile background could more readily grasp and apply. The initial proclamation, "Christ died—was raised—is coming again," for example, became "He was with God—became man—ascended to the right hand of God," thus fitting the Greek cosmological framework (Phil. 2:6-11; 1 Tim. 3:16).

It was made to speak, too, to the persistent fear of the powers of evil. In Christ, as Paul expressed it, God dealt the powers of evil a mighty blow. You need fear them no longer. He has even vanquished the last enemy of human existence, death (1 Cor. 15:54-57). He has ransomed us, as it were, like slaves from their masters (Gal. 4:5) and adopted us as children. He has restored us to a relationship with God that God intended from the first, overcoming the chasm that separated us (Rom. 5:8-11). Indeed, he guaranteed the acquittal of the guilty who trust him for their justification, becoming himself both judge and advocate. He has liberated us so that we can *do* what is right (Rom. 6:15-23).

It is in the area of application, of course, that the apostles' teaching raises the most difficulties and thence requires the greatest persistence. These difficulties emerge not merely from interpretation of the teaching in its original milieu but much more from its application in widely different milieus. Indeed, as the first chapter of this book indicated, we now live in a culture that is undergoing constant and rapid change. As culture changes, our interpretation and application of the apostles' teaching also changes. The more rapid and radical the changes, the more difficult our adjustment of its implications. It is unquestionable that a major factor in the moral ambivalence of the moment is rapidity of change.

This kind of adjustment in interpretation and application is admittedly risky and even frightening. To make it less risky, the churches have made use of confessions of faith to measure its adaptations. The most adaptable persons or groups have usually been those who felt secure in an attachment to a stake which they had driven in and around which they could move without too much apprehension of getting lost. In the end we cannot resolve all of the problems that can be posed for belief. Instead, we lay down a set of prelogical suppositions based on revelation in the confidence that God has not left himself without some witness.

Persistence in Fellowship

The second element in the Lucan formula for vitality in mission is persistence in fellowship. The English word *fellowship* scarcely does justice to the Greek word *koinonia* as used in this context. Literally *koinonia* means "sharing, having in common, participation." For the Jerusalem community *koinonia* originated out of a common experience, an experience of the resurrected Christ, of the Spirit, of divine love. From that experience emerged the community manifested in sharing of possessions and acts of charity (Acts 4:32-37).

It would not be out of place, perhaps, to contrast this understanding of community of goods with the Marxist model based on Acts 2 and 4. In Marxist theory the classless society, where goods are distributed "from each according to his (her) ability to each according to his (her) need," comes at the end and as the goal of a deliberate plan. Before it comes the dictatorship of the proletariat. In theory this dictatorship imposes proper distribution until all persons in the society recognize their mutual responsibility; then it disappears. In actuality the state owns everything and allows individuals the use of some goods. To this date, there is no evidence in any Marxist society that the dictatorship will ever cease; and it is highly questionable whether individuals can have much freedom there.

In the Lucan portrayal of the Jerusalem community, sharing of goods arose out of a deep experience of divine love (*agape*). Although Christians in Jerusalem practiced community of goods, those at Corinth and elsewhere continued to own private property. Moreover, the two customs have existed alongside one another, evidence that community of goods never became an end in itself. Community of goods and charity, therefore, both had a deeper base—that is, in an experience of true *koinonia*, oneness in the body of Christ. Love welded people of highly diverse backgrounds and personalities into a genuine community. Individuality, however, was not effaced by the community. Indeed, Luke in no way dissembled or covered up for the fact that, alongside selfless Christians such as Barnabas, there were also selfish ones such as Ananias and Sapphira. Every human community, including the church as the advance model of a new humanity, suffers the effects of egocentrism in its members. Only divine love can create genuine *koinonia*. The object is to set forth for the world a model of the humanity coming into being.

Putting Off the Old Humanity

In Colossians 3:1-17 Paul commented on the way in which the new humanity is being born out of the old. In this age, of course, it never fully emerges. The life of Christ within us is hidden, not manifest until the end (3:3). Presently we work toward that by laying aside characteristics of the old humanity and putting on characteristics of the new. The old characteristics Paul had in mind represent excesses in areas that vitally affect interpersonal relationships—sex drive, desire for possessions, and emotion in thought or speech. He did not teach here, as did the ancient Stoics, that any drive, desire, or emotion is wrong in itself. Christianity has not concluded that reason alone should govern human actions and thoughts. There is a very appropriate place for all of these. They become problems only when they go out of control. The new humanity has ample opportunity for witness here in modern society.

Consider sexual desire. Most of us are happy to see the end of the puritanical era when sex was taboo, even dirty. A certain liberating process that occurred in recent years was wholesome. The question now is whether the pendulum has swung too far to the opposite extreme. Sex is such a common topic of conversation and indulgence that its meaning is getting lost or distorted. It has been cheapened. In the new humanity we bear witness to the appropriate fulfillment of the natural sex drive, laying aside excess and improper uses (3:5).

Consider possessions. Early Christianity never affirmed the Gnostic view that material things are evil per se. Some ascetics, it is true, went a long way in this direction; but even they did not label material

goods evil. Rather, as Paul expressed it, Christians discerned a problem not in things per se but in misuse of them by letting them
become ends in themselves and thus usurp God's place in human
life. All possessions should serve a higher end.

Unbridled acquisition is a serious problem in contemporary American society. Because of our sales and consumer orientation, we buy
and acquire not according to real needs but according to artificial
and contrived needs. John Kenneth Galbraith has pointed out in
Economics and the Public Purpose that production and consumption
no longer depends upon supply and demand. Rather, giant oligopolies
determine the products they want us to buy; then they proceed
to convince us that we need them. Subtle advertising techniques
incite our most selfish and superficial desires. Acquiring this or that,
it is suggested, will bring ultimate satisfaction. But, alas, it only
increases our appetites without bringing genuine satisfaction. The
result is an endless cycle of wanting and obtaining without corre-
sponding satisfaction. Here, perhaps, we who have found the one
thing that truly satisfies can offer guidance to others.

Consider thought and speech. Paul recognized, as the Stoics did
not, that emotion controls what we think or say as much as reason.
He did not contend in Colossians 3:8 for abandonment of emotion
and cultivation of apathy or emotionlessness. Instead, he counseled
that these be kept in control and excesses removed.

Once more, what he said spoke directly to the impatient, impulsive,
hotheaded, trigger-happy culture in which we live. The hectic pace
of life both increases emotional strain and lessens the time for deliber-
ation and reflective reaction. One evidence of the damage resulting
from uncontrolled emotion is growing child abuse.

Such practices as these, then, belong to the old humanity. They
are to be laid aside. By contrast the new humanity exhibits a wholly
different character, a Christ-endowed one in which the divisions of
the old humanity no longer have effect. To be sure, natural differences, even imperfections, remain. It is the continuing effect of
these that poses a threat to the actual existence of the new humanity.
Still, this humanity already exists and will go on developing into
the completeness of Christ's humanity. In that very development
lies the witness and work of the church. Hardly any historian will

deny, that, in the final analysis, this koinonia has proved to be one of Christianity's most vital and attractive assets.

Putting On the New Humanity

Paul specified in Colossians 3:12-17 the features that identify the new humanity and that offer valuable instruction for persons of our day, as for those of his. The most crucial is *agape* love, the chief motive for all Christian action and the pivot for Christian *koinonia.* It is, Paul said, the perfect bond, one that genuinely ties together the disparate elements of humanity (Col. 3:14). In societies fragmented and torn by innumerable divisions, what experience could be more vital? Do Christians have anything more urgent to do than to love one another even as God in Christ has loved them? Can churches do anything more to implement God's design than to be communities of love, communities that embrace all and sundry without restrictions? True, love will reach out beyond gatherings of believers in a universal servant ministry, as a later chapter will show. But love has to begin at home, in the Christian family, if it is to have an effect beyond.

The family is an image Paul liked to use to describe the new humanity created in Christ. Christ was God's Son, as it were, uniquely related to the Father. Through Christ, however, God adopted all who trust him into the same family. We are brothers and sisters and sons and daughters. The implications here are astounding. Whereas most aggregations of people arise from an already existing commonality, the "household of God" incorporates persons of the most divergent backgrounds imaginable, having only *one* thing in common—their confession of God in Christ.

We have become so accustomed to seeing some of the disparateness of the members of Christ's body that its singularity nearly escapes us. Is it not remarkable to witness *koinonia* composed of young and old, male and female, black and white, wealthy and poor, capitalist and laborer, student and teacher educated and illiterate, lender and borrower, well-clad and tattered—all calling one another brother and sister? To me it is little short of mind blowing to think that, in the ancient world, slaves and masters attended the same assemblies and addressed one another with deep familiarity as suggested by

Paul in 1 Timothy 6:1-2.

All of us are aware, of course, that the actuality falls short of the ideal. Over the centuries churches have been rent by many of the same divisions that rend human societies everywhere. Is that not to be expected, however, considering the bold, almost presumptuous, effort Christianity makes to unite all humanity into one new humanity without erasing the natural characteristics of its members? What is surprising is not that the church has often failed but that it has ever succeeded in this plan! And it has succeeded often. It succeeds often today. Everything stands against this, but it has happened. How?

The apostle spells out some specifics of the way love operates to overcome barriers in an imperfect society of imperfect human beings. He lays down three groups of characteristics of the new humanity, "God's elect" (Col. 3:12, author's translation). All three groups powerfully address contemporary needs.

The first pair is *compassion and kindness.* Both of these words have an active nuance. They suggest "gut-level" care that will result in action on behalf of others. It is precisely these qualities that seem so often absent from modern urban societies, a fact which has caused Ashley Montaigu, a noted sociologist and anthropologist, to question whether we can remain human in cities larger than a few thousand. To be sure, all of us witness, read or hear about, and participate in compassionate deeds. Simultaneously, however, we get vast numbers of reports about the opposite. Who has not heard the name of Kitty Genovese, the New York girl murdered while about forty persons watched, unwilling to turn a hand to help? Other stories could be related to document the same point, but all attest to the same thing—a desensitizing of persons to others, a loss of compassion and kindness.

Where does resensitizing begin? Does it not begin in the new humanity, where, as Paul said, there has been renewal of understanding according to the divine stamp (Col. 3:10)? Does it not begin in this family of brothers and sisters in Christ, whom natural differences would otherwise separate? Sad to say, churches often offer poor models for the rest of humankind. Through the centuries, however, they have left some notable examples of compassion and kindness. Witness, for example, those loving souls mentioned by Clement of Rome (A.D. 96) who sold themselves into servitude for a time to ransom others. Or those who divested themselves of all possessions, like Barnabas and many others, to meet needs of the poor. Or the multitudes who opened their homes to widows, orphans, the sick, the disabled, the poor.

Christian compassion and kindness have always started at home, but they have not gone unnoticed elsewhere. In the third century Tertullian of Carthage quoted pagan astonishment that before Christians even knew one another, they loved one another. It was a revealing compliment.

A second pair of characteristics that the new humanity might model is *humility and meekness.* These probably will not be easily understood or regarded as virtues in our age and culture. In contemporary parlance they suggest weakness and self-effacement, qualities difficult for persons who prize power and self-assertiveness or ambition. Indeed, since the mid-nineteenth century, Christianity has been pilloried as the enemy of human development by disciples of Marx, Nietzsche, and Freud. Such criticism has not lacked foundation in some Christian sources; but, broadly applied, it fails to grasp the proper significance of these two words. Both humility and meekness stem from a proper self-estimate. They represent the antithesis of boastfulness and pretension, which arise out of low self-esteem.

As modern transactional analysts have pointed out, it is persons who feel badly about themselves who "put on airs," to call attention to themselves. Those who feel good about themselves do not have to boast. Rather, they can accept themselves as they are. The source of this kind of self-esteem, of course, lies not in what we as human beings are in and of ourselves but in an experience of divine approval. It rests in the fact that, as Paul said elsewhere, "God shows his love for us in that while we were yet sinners Christ died for us" (Rom. 5:8). God OK'd us. He affirmed us as his own children.

Are humility and meekness, thus interpreted, not qualities to exhibit in the new humanity as a rebuke to the pride and blind ambition so characteristic of our age and culture? How sad that the latter have gripped some church leaders as powerfully as some political leaders in America. It is perhaps endemic to a social and economic system that is predicated upon competition as a chief mark. It is not that ambition is per se contrary to Christian principles; it belongs to human nature. But ambition that does not subordinate itself to some higher end is inherently unchristian and brings its own recompense, as Charles Colson and John Dean could readily attest. The obverse of this is a humility grounded in a recognition that God, not human beings, governs the world and directs it toward an ultimately meaningful end.

A third set of characteristics that the new humanity might model is *patience, forbearance, and forgiveness*. Like humility and meekness, these are not among the prized and cultivated virtues of our age and culture. On the contrary, our civilization is noted for impatience, hotheadedness, and implacability. The latter qualities are connected with the technological revolution that underlies this civilization. They result not merely from the blinding speeds and the accelerated pace of life, though these cause stresses and strains on the human psyche which can be unmanageable, but also from an accompanying exteriorization process. Our culture, as Thomas Merton accused, leaves too little room to seek wisdom for its own sake, to ponder the meaning of our activities and actions, to evaluate.

For a humanity that suffers this kind of distress, the new humanity may witness the deeper reality that lies at the base of life. When all else fails to unite a fragmented and diverse group of persons, these are essential. First, *patience*. Maintaining control is difficult in a pressure-packed society. Recently newspapers across the United States have reported grim statistics about child abuse—beatings, tortures, even murders of children. In few instances would these be the product of deliberate, planned abuse. Rather, they arise from passions not kept in control, aggravated by parental stresses more than child misbehavior. Terrorism has become increasingly common. Its sources are complex, but a major factor is surely an unwillingness to wait for solutions to problems that might delay too long.

Second, *forbearance*. The phrase the apostle used here says literally, "holding up with one another." This concept recognizes that hurts, offenses, and injuries will occur, that they are unavoidable even in the emerging new humanity. When they do occur, the tendency of most of us will be to react quickly in anger and to defend ourselves impetuously. Love says, "Hold up a while! Wait until you have had time to look the situation over more carefully." We will not always find the situation changed when we have held up for a time, but our attitudes and reactions will often change. As a result, we can maintain the integrity of fellowship, whether of a family or a church or another type of community, *despite imperfections and faults.*

Third, *forgiveness.* When even patience and forbearance fail, there is need of forgiveness. Forgiveness, too, is an uncommon practice in modern society. Actually, most of us are more adept at retaliation. We have devised numerous ways to pay others back for offenses they have committed—a glance, a word, a voice inflection, a motion of the hand, gossip, physical violence, and more fully devised strategies of revenge. The ancient law of retaliation, "eye for eye, tooth for tooth" (Ex. 21:24; Lev. 24:20; Deut. 19:21), still seems to make the most sense to most persons and societies. Each should have his or her due.

Several years ago *Reader's Digest* carried a story illustrative of the subtlety of human ability to repay. A husband and wife attended a party. All evening long the wife and the hostess exchanged the most glowing compliments. "How lovely your dress is." "Oh, isn't it wonderful your husband got this new promotion?" "How marvelous to hear your children are doing so well in school." After the party, as the couple entered their home, the wife blurted out, "I *hate* that woman!" All the compliments were only a cover-up for a tooth and claw attack on one another, not by *what* was said but by the *way* it was said.

Agape love does not retaliate. It turns the other cheek, gives two coats to a person who demands one, walks a second mile, and lends without expectation of repayment (Matt. 5:38-42). It flows out to the offender in reconciliation. Indeed, Jesus admonished those making an offering in the Temple to seek first reconciliation with offended persons before leaving the offering (Matt. 5:24). Efforts at reconciliation, most of us know from experience, will sometimes fail and even be misunderstood; even God's efforts to reconcile errant humanity have. We persevere, nevertheless, because it is the nature of *agape* not to relent. Only so can *koinonia* emerge out of a fragmented and disparate humanity.

This lengthy discussion should have clarified why it is necessary to *persevere* in the apostles' fellowship. *Koinonia* will not arise automatically. Even though it belonged to God's purpose for humanity from the beginning, it has been frustrated by human disobedience, by the human tendency to usurp God's place in the order of things. The new humanity, Christ its head and firstfruit, is going about the task of restoring this relationship by modeling *koinonia* born of divine love.

Persistence in the Breaking of Bread and Prayers

The final element in the Lucan formula for vitality in mission is persistence in "the breaking of bread and prayers." This phrase refers, I judge, to worship. The early Christians worshiped in a variety of ways. Until A.D. 70 most Jewish Christians in Palestine continued to frequent the Temple. Outside of Palestine, until expelled, they attended synagogues. From the first, however, they also gathered in Christian homes for a fellowship meal ("breaking of bread") combined with the symbolic meal we now call the Lord's Supper (1 Cor. 11:17-34) and for prophetic services such as that described by Paul in 1 Corinthians 14. What differentiated the Christian special observances from others was a sense of joyous confidence and expectation generated by belief that the risen Christ was present with his followers in the Spirit and would return shortly to consummate his purposes for them.

The most serious error made by some proponents of radical or secular theology in the sixties was to contend that such worship was not vital to—indeed, stood in the way of—the church's mission. It is true that we may dispense with various *forms* of worship. As suggested in the preceding chapter, Christianity's very existence is not tied to particular forms. Moreover, most of us would be happy to bury lifeless and lackluster liturgies, perfunctory prayers, senseless songs, and meaningless mouthing of words in sermons—all of which we suffer through often enough. To abandon worship altogether because it lacks something, however, is a wrongheaded approach to the problem. That would be pulling the plug, as it were, from the socket that supplies current for the church's mission. What is needed is not abandonment of worship but greater persistence in it. Persistence is required precisely because we worship inadequately.

How do we enhance our worship? From historical study I have concluded that style or form is less significant than attitude and intention in worship. The diversity of early Christian styles of worship at least allows room for the kind of experimentation in worship that went on during the fifties and sixties in the United States and will continue to be tried in "the third world" for decades. The fact that Christian worship of God centers around a personal covenant with God effected through Christ, however, will necessitate a christological focus and continuing observance of the symbol of this covenant, the Lord's Supper. Beyond this, the crucial factors lie in attitude and intention.

Prayer

Attitude and intention are reflected, first, in individuals and their receptivity to God's leading. For several decades western authors both inside and outside the church have been calling attention to God's seeming absence. Human beings wait, but God never comes, as Samuel Beckett expressed the human plight in his play *Waiting for Godot*. This problem has been analyzed both as a God problem and as a human problem.

For those who see it as a God problem, the experience of God's absence is due to the fact that (1) God does not exist and never has, except in human imagination (Bertrand Russell), (2) God once existed but no longer does so (F. Nietzsche, Thomas J. J. Altizer, William Hamilton), or (3) he has gone into hiding (Karl Barth). For those who see it as a human problem, as I do, it is due to the development of an outlook and style of life which has caused not merely problems of belief but, much more, a withering of human capacity to commune and converse with God. If the former answer is correct, there is nothing human beings can do to correct the situation. If the latter answer is correct, there is something they can do: They can cultivate the capacity for prayer.

By prayer I do not mean words or thoughts that we put together to inform God about our situation. In public worship, of course, we will use words and thoughts; but these are only vehicles. Prayer itself is communion, communication, or conversation between ourselves as personal beings and God as the ultimate personal reality in the universe. By this definition prayer means not just telling but also listening. Most persons, since they learn to pray through participation in public worship, have practiced prayer as telling—but they have done little about listening. Yet if we heed the teaching of the Old Testament Psalms or Jesus about prayer, God is always beaming messages to us through creation, other persons, experiences we have, or directly. These teach us that God is "nearer to us than we are to ourselves," that he is inescapably near, and that he cares.

Therefore, we do not need to pile up words like nonbelievers; the Father knows what we need before we ask (Matt. 6:7-8). To do so is an expression of littleness of faith. And this littleness of faith is the cause of anxiety and dread of life. We can learn from the lilies, the birds, and the hairs of our head how much the Father cares (Matt. 6:25-34). From the example of human fatherhood we can ask God, knowing that he, like a human parent, will do what is best, even if not as we ask (Matt. 7:7-12).

An essential preparation for genuine and vital worship will be persistence in prayer. The apostle Paul enjoined the Thessalonians to pray incessantly (1 Thess. 5:17). He surely did not mean by that that they were to withdraw into a hermitage or monastery in order to say prayers. He meant, rather, that they should maintain constant communion with the heavenly Father who stands at our heart's door, waiting to be invited in. He meant that they should "practice the presence of God" in whatever they were doing. He meant that their daily conversation with God in the interior, in the heart, should inform and orient and guide their activities—all of them. Those who maintain this kind of intimate communion will bring something vital to public worship.

Have Christians in the modern day taken their responsibility here with adequate seriousness? Or does the growth of interest in oriental religions, Transcendental Meditation, yoga, and numerous prayer forms testify that the churches have taught too little about the focal element of religion? Can we expect vitality in public worship and ministry until we learn how to pray?

Vital Public Worship

Although this is not an essay about public worship, it will be useful to consider further the issue of vitality in public worship. In the last analysis, of course, it is the living God who, through his Spirit, produces this vitality. It is he who addresses us, his people, as we gather and renew our covenant with him. In prayer, song, sermon, and other words he instructs, informs, admonishes, rebukes, chastizes, exhorts, and encourages us. In some special way perhaps he meets us there and delivers his Word. True worship, therefore, depends on God's inescapable presence.

At the same time, however, vitality depends also on our receptiveness. God does not violate the inner space of those whom he has made in his image. He respects their individuality; thus, he enters only by invitation into their inner sanctuaries. He stands at the door knocking, waiting to be invited in.

One does not have to do an exhaustive study to see that much modern worship fails to establish a meeting place between God and his people. All too often loudness and activity are taken as the measures of vitality, and the true measure is neglected altogether. The true measure is how deeply this gathering results in reaffirmation and renewal of the covenant between God and his people. Symbolic *liturgeia* (service) should result in actual *liturgeia!* Our worship should furnish us with a vision of what God is doing in his world and challenge us to join him in that task.

Viewed from the angle of covenant making between God and people, worship might be more vital if we kept in mind the following considerations:

1. *That the covenant is based on God's mighty acts on behalf of us.* For the old covenant the crucial act is his rescuing of Israel from Egyptian bondage through Moses; for the new it is his rescuing of all humanity from servitude to sin through Jesus. Insofar as our worship is concerned, this means that we need faithfully to portray those acts through which God rescued us. Liturgically oriented Christians may do a better job of this than those of nonliturgical or antiliturgical slant. The great liturgies of Christianity sought to incorporate the story of salvation, particularly through a Christian

calendar which could highlight the "great moments" in the history
of salvation. In Orthodox churches icon screens do the same thing.
Nonliturgical services rely more on spontaneity and thus do not recall
the history of salvation systematically. The result is often a one-sided
emphasis upon favorite parts of the story.

In this same area it is important to recall that, from the first
century on, the Lord's Supper has been the symbol par excellence
of the greatest of God's mighty acts. If many liturgically oriented
Christians have sometimes turned this observance into a kind of fetish,
nonliturgical Christians have sometimes glossed over and erased its
meaning altogether. In this day of revolution in media we are redis-
covering the importance and effectiveness of symbols in com-
municating truth. An acted parable, such as the Lord's Supper is,
may engage each of us in a way merely hearing the spoken word
cannot. In the Lord's Supper we do not merely *depict* Jesus' death
and resurrection. We also act out our participation in the servant
role which he played and is playing through his body, the church.
The Jewish *Mishnah*, the codified oral tradition, contains an instructive illustration of this point. It directed observers of the Passover
meal as follows: *"In every generation a man must so regard himself
as if he came forth out of Egypt."* [2]

2. *That the covenant has two sides—God's and ours.* This means
that worship should present an opportunity for a vital encounter
between the worshipers and God. Here is where nonliturgical Christians probably possess some insights from which liturgical Christians
might learn. If the former sometimes go to extremes in informality
and spontaneity, the latter sometimes bog down in ritualism and
formalism. Admittedly both liturgical and nonliturgical services fall
into ruts from which they cannot escape, but the former does so
more often than the latter. In the sermon at least the latter keep
alive the prophetic note, God's demand, and call for a response.
Although justifiable criticism may be made of actual practice, invitations in Baptist churches in America to respond to the word by
commitment or renewal of the covenant are doubtless an authentic
way of manifesting this response. The earliest Christian preaching,
at any rate, included such appeals.

More can still be done, however, in nonliturgical churches to engage all persons in the act of praising, thanking, confessing, petitioning, interceding, and blessing God. In many churches too much of the act of worship falls on the shoulders of one person, the pastor. The problem we are faced with here is that the members of the body listen but otherwise scarcely participate. Here we might learn again from liturgical Christians, for the liturgies *require* participation by all. The earliest extant liturgy, recorded by Justin Martyr circa A.D. 150, shows extensive lay participation. This liturgy included the following elements:

> Readings from both the Old and New Testaments
> Homily by the "president" (apparently the bishop or pastor)
> Prayer by the congregation while standing
> Presentation of the offering of bread and wine mixed with water and foodstuffs for the needy (elements brought by members)
> Prayers and thanksgiving by the "president"
> "Amen!" ("So be it!") by the congregation
> Distribution to all present
> Sharing of the symbolic meal by all
> Delivery of the offering (food) to those who were sick or in prison by the deacons
> Collection of money for the needy

The striking feature of this liturgy was the amount of lay participation. Lay persons read scriptures, offered prayer, presented their offering, participated in the Lord's Supper, and gave to the needy. At only two points—the sermon and the prayer to consecrate bread and wine—did the clergy assume a major role.

3. *That the covenant is ultimately a personal one.* This brings us again to the issue of attitude and intention. No liturgy or absence of liturgy can assure authentic encounter between God and his people unless their hearts are open and receptive to it. Because they stand in a highly visible position, leaders will be a model, whether good or bad. By their reverence for God in manner of life they will set a tone for piety. We may use varied forms and styles. One thing we cannot compromise, however, is authenticity in personal commitment of those who lead. That can be contagious.

9
The People of God
on Mission

Thus far we have emphasized being the church, the new humanity, the body of Christ. Such an accent recognizes that the church fulfills its mission first through gathering to be furbished in the apostles' teaching, fellowship, and worship. This is not merely preparation for mission; it *is* mission! For the gathering of disparate members into one body, one new humanity, is in itself a goal of the church. And the *koinonia* that exists in the church, as history shows, exerts a powerful attraction.

At this juncture we will turn to examine images that speak more directly of the outward thrust of Christianity, its discharging of its mission in and to the world. The image whose implications we will draw out in this chapter, that of the people of God, contains certain definite suggestions about the way in which the church may discharge this mission through proclamation and priesthood. Before looking at these two facets of the mission, however, it will be worthwhile to examine two different historical approaches to doing it.

Two Approaches to Mission

The National Model

One approach, envisioned by the Hebrew people in ancient times and again in modern times, is to develop a nation that would exemplify God's name and purpose in its corporate life. The promise to Abraham was that God would make of him (and his people) "a great nation" that would bless all nations (Gen. 12:1-3). As the Hebrew people came out of Egypt under Moses' leadership, national consciousness grew still more firm. It was *as a nation* that Israel would honor God's name among the Gentiles, being holy because

Yahweh is holy (Lev. 11:44-45; 19:2; 20:7), not holy as individuals but as a nation (Ex. 19:6).

In the period of the monarchy the prophets fulminated against the failure of Israel to be a holy nation—that is, set apart from the other Palestinian peoples—thus bringing dishonor upon the name of God. As a nation, they went "awhoring" after other gods, despite being God's chosen people (Hos. 2:2-3). Thus God allowed them to be vanquished by other nations and carried off into captivity. In the exilic period the author of Isaiah 40—55 urged faithfulness so that God would return his people home and they would again proclaim his virtues through their national integrity (43:21).

Through substantial periods of history Christians, too, have followed the national model in mission. The first nation to adopt Christianity as the national faith was Armenia (A.D. 300). Subsequently national adoption occurred in the Roman Empire, in Ethiopia, among numerous barbarian peoples in Europe during the Middle Ages, in the so-called Holy Roman Empire, in many other states of Europe as they developed, and even in the early American colonies. All of these nations emulated the Old Testament model of a commonwealth in which civil and religious affairs were considered one.

Similar thinking about the mission of Israel has revived in modern times in the Zionist movement. As many Jewish people have returned to their homeland, they have again envisioned themselves fulfilling the historic mission of Israel by developing a nation based upon Old Testament principles. In their nation, even though the majority of the people are secular, they seek fully to integrate religious observances with civil affairs in such a way that the biblical principles of justice and mercy will be exemplified. In one nation, moreover, they believe they represent a unity of diverse peoples of the earth.

The Diaspora Model

The other approach to the mission of the people of God arose during the Diaspora of the Jewish people from their homeland (722 B.C. and after). Out of necessity the witness of Israel occurred not as a nation, which no longer existed, but among the peoples. The focal point of Jewish worship was no longer the Temple but the synagogue, which attracted God-fearers and made converts to Israel.

By the time of Jesus Judaism had developed a vigorous witness among the scattered peoples of the earth (Matt. 23:15). In Alexandria a Jew named Philo put together a strong apologetic for Judaism based on the Old Testament.

Christianity also adopted this model. Indeed, the split between early Christianity and its parent religion resulted from a dispute over incorporation of Gentiles into the people of God without insisting on Jewish "marks" such as circumcision of males. Not until A.D. 300 could Christians anywhere think of doing mission as a nation. Instead, as we observed earlier, they discharged their mission largely by planting churches wherever they went and gathering people of all nations into them. Inevitably this meant adapting to the customs of different peoples while holding onto certain essential marks of Christianity. But Christians zealously sought to bear witness to God, whom they had come to know in Jesus Christ.

In the modern day Christians have again found themselves in a Diaspora situation. Christian nations, if such ever existed, have ceased to exist. It is the United States, however, that the pursuit of the Diaspora model has born its finest fruit. Given immense pluralism and separation of church and state from early in American history, the churches have had to employ voluntary means to win converts. They have not been able to rely on state assistance or a pattern of parishes. Instead, local congregations and denominations have devised their own plans for effecting the mission of the people of God.

An Assessment

Each of these models has strengths and weaknesses. The national model allows for better integration of faith and life. Within a nation all persons and even institutions can operate under one religious perspective. One problem with it is that, as often happened in the past, the merger of civil and religious affairs may lead to religious oppression. If one religious view is strongly enforced, there is no room for nonconformity. Another is that, today, few nations represent Christianity or any other faith as their faith; most are pluralistic and secular.

The Diaspora model, while not integrating faith and life as well, allows for meeting the challenge of pluralism and secularity. Indeed, viewed from this perspective, the goal is not national but universal witness of the people of God. Instead of maintaining an ultimate loyalty to one state, therefore, Christians pledge allegiance to a kingdom not of this world (John 18:36). They can accept pluralism and even a minority status as facts of life by putting religion on a voluntary basis. Admittedly one might often wish for an entire nation to act on consistent religious principles, but the American experiment in voluntarism has not worked badly.

Proclamation

Scattered among the diverse peoples of the earth, the people of God may discharge their mission in a variety of ways. One of these is proclamation. In the words of 1 Peter 2:9, alluding to Isaiah 43:21, those not a people have become God's people, "that you may declare the wonderful deeds of him who called you out of darkness into his marvelous light."

Embodiment of a Message

The question that arises immediately is: How do we proclaim the mighty acts of God? One method that we should not overlook or minimize is embodiment in conduct or life-style. In the section just cited, for instance, Peter commanded his readers to "maintain good conduct among the Gentiles, so that . . . they may see your good deeds and glorify God on the day of visitation" (1 Pet. 2:12). Many other early writers seconded his motion. And through nearly twenty centuries of history the effectiveness of the Christian proclamation has depended to a great degree upon this formula. Deeds have to match words! Otherwise, words become nothing but "a tale told by an idiot, full of sound and fury, signifying nothing."

To a large degree, of course, as Adolf Harnack once observed about early Christianity, the Christian mission is a moral enterprise, representing holiness and love. The proof of Christianity lies not in *claims* to transform people but in actual transformation of them. By about A.D. 200 Christians began to receive some high compliments in this regard. Critics begrudgingly admitted that Christianity taught simple, relatively uneducated folk to live and die like philosophers.

Even when some ridiculed Christian doctrine, they could not deny the proof that lay in the product.

Conversely, Christianity has suffered censure, rebuke, and rejection when deeds have not matched words. We need not suppose, of course, that any generation has embodied the message in a faultless way. Certainly the first generations did not. Paul, for instance, had to rebuke the Corinthians for tolerating an incestuous relationship "of a kind that is not found even among pagans" (1 Cor. 5:1). Such cases turned up in other communities and ages. While they have not destroyed the Christian witness, they have impeded it more than once.

A fourth-century Roman historian named Ammianus Marcellinus, for example, scarcely veiled his utter contempt for a religion that produced wrangling over high offices as Christianity did. Ammianus commented about the Emperor Julian's plan to replace Christianity with a restoration of paganism that he did not have to fear a united population, "knowing as he did from experience that no wild beasts are such enemies to mankind as are most of the Christians in their deadly hatred of one another." [1] To this comment one could add many sad tales of persecution and fighting throughout the centuries, perhaps reaching a peak as a result of the Protestant Reformation.

In our own day the churches have undergone severe criticism for their failure to match their words with deeds. Many such criticisms have been blanket attacks on anything and everything the churches do, obviously reflecting exaggerations growing out of more specific griefs suffered. Behind them, however, lay some real lapses. While claiming to represent a God of love and reconciliation, for instance, many congregations have barred their doors to people of other races. In a matter so central to the nature of the church itself—that is, as a fellowship incorporating all humanity—the churches followed rather than led others. Moreover, many still have a long way to go before they catch up with the United States Supreme Court decision of 1954, which invalidated the principle of segregation.

It is not merely in the transcending of racial barriers, however, that many of the churches have failed to live up to their own nature. They reflect also society's rifts with respect to wealth, age, sex, and numerous other matters. Like racial prejudice, other prejudices intrude so subtly that many persons do not know they have them. Here are two examples.

One Sunday morning a middle-aged man dressed in overalls walked down the aisle of a middle-class church in Louisville. He sat in the seat occupied every Sunday by a prominent banker and his wife. All those present did an "eyes right" and silently asked, "What's *he* doing here?" The men pondered those labels on their inside lapel pockets—Hart, Schaffner, and Marx or Austin Leeds. They looked at the bib on the this man's overalls. Plain as day, the label read Lee. Without meaning to, the whole group communicated that this man wasn't "our kind." He never returned again.

On another occasion a youth in his late teens came. He had shoulder-length hair and a beard, both neatly trimmed. He wore a maroon corduroy jacket, a gold turtleneck sweater, and purple trousers. After the service one of the faithful, longtime members leaned over and whispered quite audibly to another person, "What's *he* doing here?" The irony of the question was the young man's face was the spitting image of Salman's head of Christ! This youth came two Sundays but no more.

Other stories could be related. Citing such isolated instances, however, gives an unbalanced and inaccurate picture of what happens in the churches. Despite such sad distortions as these, the churches have also exhibited divine love and even holiness. They are at worst guilty only of compiling a mixed record, which perhaps is to be expected. The church is, after all, never a pure body but always a mixed one, as Augustine argued against the ancient Donatists. Whatever holiness and love the church exhibits depends on God, not the members of the body. Because it is composed of human beings, the church should readily admit its weakness.

Indeed, one thing that historical study doubtless confirms about the Christian mission to Paul's confession that "we are not sufficient of ourselves, to be considered anything of ourselves, but our sufficiency is from God" (2 Cor. 3:6, author's translation). Christianity surely has registered whatever success it has had by means of "earthen vessels" in order "to show that the transcendent power belongs to God and not to us" (2 Cor. 4:7).

Over and over again failures, considered from a human perspective, turned out to be successes, and successes at best mixed successes or even failures. Christianity began, remember, with a failure, the crucifixion of its founder. The mission to the Jews failed. Yet these "failures" forced the mission to expand to the Roman world, where Christianity had astounding success. On the other hand, the conversion of Constantine, which appeared to the majority of early Christians as a signal for the dawning of the millennium, cost an immense amount in state interference in church affairs and decay of Christian discipline through too-rapid conversions.

Conceding its humanity, the church still should strive to bear witness to God by embodying his holiness and love. Although as the people of God we will always fall short of the mark, we can surrender ourselves to the one who must infuse his holiness and love into us. In this way alone can we become instruments of his saving grace. The word continues in the flesh. It comes not merely as word but as power (2 Cor. 4:7).

Oral Proclamation: Is It Needed?

Some Christians might halt a discussion of proclamation at this point. In the liturgical traditions, for example, there has been a tendency to emphasize embodiment of the Word in the Eucharist and thus to de-emphasize oral proclamation. This outlook goes back to the third and fourth centuries, during which the Eucharist came to serve as the center of the service of the faithful. As long as all persons in an area were professing Christians, of course, this custom made sense. But it was not adequate for the evangelization of new areas or for the revitalization of faith in old ones. Not surprisingly, therefore, oral proclamation gained in importance as faith deteriorated in Europe during the late Middle Ages. Orders devoted specifically to preaching, such as the Dominicans, arose around 1200 in imitation of lay preaching movements. These played a significant part in crusades to win both errant Christians and non-Christians.

The most serious shift in the place of preaching occurred, however, in connection with the Protestant Reformation. Caught in a dramatic change in understanding concerning the way in which knowledge is appropriated as a result of the invention of movable type in 1456, the reformers elevated preaching above sacrament. Subsequently, the latter has held pride of place in most of the Protestant churches, while the Eucharist has done so in the Catholic churches.

In recent years, however, a curious exchange of emphases has taken place. At the Second Vatican Council the Roman Church elevated preaching to a much higher level in regular services of worship than it had held for centuries. Meanwhile, during the sixties, many Protestants began to lose confidence in preaching, considering it an outmoded aspect of Christian observance. The chief source of such skepticism was probably doubt about the propriety of winning converts. The mission of Christianity was seen much more often in terms of social service and social action. Exponents of radical or secular theology doubted even whether anything should differentiate a Christian from any other person. In addition, church attendance declined, unable, many supposed, to compete with the media and other sources of guidance or entertainment.

Happily, preaching has enjoyed a recovery in the seventies, assisted no doubt by the deeper examination of its values that came with the skepticism of the sixties. After the early skepticism subsided, it was found that people still responded to effective oral proclamation. Moreover, modern electronic media, far from hampering preaching, could aid it. What was needed was not a completely new form for disseminating the good news but adaptation of an old one. This adaptation could occur vis-à-vis content, style, time, and place of proclamation, as it frequently has in the past.

The Adaptation of Proclamation

Content. The Christian message is not a static one. Rather, the Word repeatedly "becomes flesh" in varied cultures and times. Already in the New Testament era, as we noted in an earlier chapter, this message took on two essentially different forms, one for Jews and the other for Gentiles. It has done the same many times subsequently as Christianity has entered other cultures and nations. Indeed, Christianity's most serious failures—for example, in the Far East—have occurred when missionaries did not sufficiently adapt this message. There are obviously limits to which this accommodation can go, but we need not fear abandonment of essentials as long as we keep in touch continuously with the historical events in which

God discloses himself and his purpose.

In the present day western culture possesses a crazy-quilt pattern that challenges the ingenuity of Christianity's apologists and preachers. No single form of the message will reach all persons. To be effective, therefore, we will have to put it into a number of different wrappings.

A traditional wrap obviously satisfies many persons, for conservative, more or less biblically literalist, churches attract large numbers. This is due to matters other than their message, but it is unquestionable that their conservative message supplies what many persons wish to hear. The same fact helps to explain the sustained success of Billy Graham, Oral Roberts, and a number of other popular evangelists.

A growing number of persons, however, are not content with repetition of ancient verities. They want a faith that will speak to the modern life and outlook. For them this means an adaptation of the gospel message to several modern perspectives. One is the *scientific outlook,* which pervades our thoughts so completely. Instead of attacking the evolutionary model of science, some have tried to show how faith in a personal God can still be fitted into this framework. The Bible affirms that God directs this process; it does not tell how. To affirm evolution is not to deny God, therefore.

Indeed, it is possible, as the Jesuit paleontologist and philosopher Teilhard de Chardin has shown, to explain faith in terms of evolution. This process has moved forward and upward not by chance but because of a "pull" from God. In Jesus of Nazareth God has given us a window to see where the process is going. As humanity is the arrow pointing the way to the ultimate goal of evolution, so Christ is the arrow within the arrow. Ultimately, as Paul affirmed, God will be "all in all" (1 Cor. 15:28).

Another modern perspective to which some have addressed the gospel is what is called *existentialism.* Existentialism involves a quest for meaning in a world that has lost meaning as a result of cataclysmic events, especially two world wars in quick succession. Existentialists have insisted that the individual would find meaning only by separating from the crowd and ultimately by willing his or her own death. It is easy to see how Jesus' pronouncement of the inbreak of the kingdom of God and call for self-denial and crossbearing could correspond to such a plea. Following Jesus would entail willing one's own death.

A third modern perspective, related to the preceding ones to which the gospel has been addressed, is the *pessimism and near nihilism* of the modern era. Curiously, the most significant response has grown out of a Christian-Marxist dialogue going on in Europe. Marxists have recognized, as Christians have done for centuries, that no society can progress without some vision of the future. Christian theologians have responded with a theology of hope, which recognizes that the present earthly existence is never final; it points always toward something greater.

Style. Just as the message itself can be adapted, so also can the style. This kind of adaptation, too, has taken place from the beginning of Christianity. For Jewish audiences the first missionaries relied on proof texts from the Scriptures and the use of stories to get their message across. For Gentile audiences they gradually developed sermons that imitated Greek rhetorical style, depending more on rational argument. Early Protestant preaching recovered some of the freshness of early Christian preaching. In a century, however, it had bogged down in a pedantic rhetorical style meant to impress rather than to persuade or aid. In reaction to this, about 1975, Philip Jakob Spener, father of Pietism, urged the cultivation of more practical and less rhetorical preaching. During the Great Awakening in the American colonies, about 1726-1742, preachers introduced more emotional appeals and practical, everyday applications.

Preaching is in the process of another change of style as a result of developments in modern means of communication and the breakdown of authority models of the past. The media themselves now serve as major channels for proclamation, but they can never replace the direct communication that occurs in the gathering of the people of God. The gospel is, after all, a personal message borne best by persons.

What the media have done more than anything is to alter the manner of preaching. A preacher, for example, no longer needs a stentorian voice like George Whitefield's, which could be distinctly heard, according to Benjamin Franklin, a quarter-mile away. He can rely on electronic gadgets to assist him. At the same time, he has to give more attention to visual effects. More importantly, however, his tone, while not exactly conversational, may suffer if it is too authoritarian. Indeed, one of the growing features of contemporary communication is its dialogical character. The more an audience can be brought into the sermon as participants, the better. This does not mean that someone besides the preacher will speak, although actual pulpit dialogues are sometimes used effectively. It means, rather, that the preacher will seek to lead his or her hearers along the path he/she has trod.

An important element of biblical faith that coalesces with modern temperament is that it is based on testimony and storytelling, the sharing of experience. Contemporary audiences like for the speaker to share personal experiences. Although sharing may go to ridiculous extremes, it can be done tastefully in ways that may aid others. It is wise, however, to seek a balance of approaches and not to allow one to dominate.

Time. Time of proclamation may also vary, as it has in the past. The first Christians, for instance, observed the Jewish calendar, meeting on Saturday night after 6 P.M. when the first day of the week began. As more and more Gentiles entered the church, they shifted to the Roman calendar, meeting very early on Sunday morning. They did not observe Sunday as a holiday until the time of Constantine. In the Middle Ages the church itself arranged the clock and the calendar.

The radical upheaval in European and American social patterns which is labeled secularization means that the church no longer sets clock or calendar. The latter are determined, rather, by what we might call the economic system—business and industry. Once again, consequently, the churches find themselves compelled to accommodate the clock and the calendar of modern society. They can no longer count on the long-observed custom of no business competition on Sunday, for example, to encourage attendance at the usual hours. Nor can they expect industries to close so that all members will be likely to attend. Instead, they find themselves adjusting days and hours to have an opportunity to proclaim the good news.

There is no problem, of course, in adapting either clock or calendar.

The good news can be announced anytime or anywhere. It is true that Christians have regarded Sunday, the first day of the week, as having special significance as a day of worship. That is because the resurrection and Jesus' first appearances occurred on that day. Christians, therefore, will always attach special importance to this day. This special time, however, need not preclude proclamation at other times or places. The limit of adaptation will be the needs of people and the inventiveness of leaders.

Place. Finally, the place of proclamation may also change. The first Christians went various places to proclaim the good news—temple, synagogue, homes, the street, the countryside. Not until the era of peace beginning with the Emperor Gallienus, around A.D. 260, could they safely begin to build special buildings designed for worship; and not until after Constantine's conversion could they build these everywhere in the empire. In time the whole of Europe came to be divided into parishes.

The urbanization of European and American society since the late Middle Ages no longer allows the churches to depend upon established places for dissemination of their message. Some churches, especially in residential areas, will continue to serve as the chief location for proclamation. Local residents still gather there as in the past. However, in large metropolises an increasing number of persons do not seek churches; the churches have to seek them and find ways to enlist them.

One approach that seems to work effectively in secularized Europe is "house churches." Believers gather in homes for Bible study, prayer, worship, and witness. Often persons who would not otherwise attend larger church gatherings will participate in the more relaxed and informal worship of a home. In Rome, Italy, where I served as interim pastor of Rome Baptist church, devout lay persons have organized numerous Bible study groups, meeting at many different times, to supplement the church's outreach. Little by little, I found, they lead the uncommitted toward the larger fellowship.

Another approach is through the media—radio and television. This is often costly, and its effects are difficult to measure; but many persons may have their only connection with the Christian church in this way. Since the media are employed so forcefully and effectively in promotion today, it is inevitable that the churches will use them for their promotion. There is always some risk of distorting the Christian proclamation because popular advertising concentrates its appeals upon gut-level desires and needs. Christian appeals made in the same way could easily pervert and distort fundamental principles and values of Christianity. Taking care to avoid such distortions, however, Christians might employ the media to reach persons and to inculcate Christian truths.

A third approach, less effective now than in an earlier day, is community-wide evangelistic efforts. Together churches of a community can muster efforts that would fail if undertaken individually. Massive attendance at Billy Graham rallies proves that such cooperative effort still has possibilities. The most crucial aspects of such rallies are marshalling of effort prior to the actual meeting and the postrevival follow-up.

A fourth approach, enjoying a resurgence with sects like Hare Krishna and the Moonies, is individual witness at busy thoroughfares such as airports. The Hare Krishnasts and the Moonies station attractive young persons in airports to hand out tracts, make a personal pitch for their faith, gather offerings, and otherwise convey their message.

These four approaches represent only a small portion of the possibilities. Like its Founder, the church will have to go wherever people are, bearing its message of love, joy, peace, and all the rest.

Priesthood

The other major dimension of the mission of the people of God is a priestly one. Our priesthood is essentially a sharing in Christ's reconciling work. In Christ, as Paul says, God was reconciling the world to himself. So we, as ambassadors of Christ, make our appeal to others to be reconciled to God (2 Cor. 5:19-20). We appeal also for them to be reconciled with one another.

This priestly ministry is one that goes on all the time, both within and outside the Christian congregation. The task is never finished, even within the church, because, as we have noted earlier, the fragmentation of the old humanity still pervades the new. The church thus has thrust upon it the challenging job of mediating between

God and human beings and between human beings and other human beings. Let us explore some ways in which we may perform this task.

Reconcilers Between God and Human Beings

Through his life and death, Christ has already accomplished the work of reconciliation. Through him, as the apostle Paul says, we have now obtained reconciliation (Rom. 5:11). We, therefore, are ministers, mediators, or instruments of this reconciliation, seeking first to help our fellows find themselves in relationship to God. How can we do this?

Our priesthood would seem to begin with helping people find the meaning of life in Jesus Christ, bringing them the fullness of life, helping them discover themselves. This is not as simple as the old clichés "winning the lost to Christ" or "saving souls" imply. It involves, rather, an extensive priestly ministry of the church through which an individual becomes a wholesome, well-integrated person within the context of the society in which he or she lives.

This, of course, means that we cannot take our responsibility in evangelism lightly. It is not enough simply to wrest a confession from someone in order to say we have done our part. Genuine Christian evangelism requires the cultivation of a relationship with a person through which we bring him or her into a personal relationship with Christ. Impersonal evangelism offends. What can be more offensive than for a complete stranger to ask one about the most intimate matter in his or her life? Yet much would-be evangelism today takes that form. A stranger from the local church rings the doorbell of a neighborhood home, invites himself or herself in, and proceeds to ask about another's eternal salvation. Small wonder he/she gets a rebuff and a family is driven further from the church! Small wonder also that lay persons have balked at pleas for personal witnessing!

As we face a more and more secular era, there may be a more natural and more personal witness that we can recover or develop. The simple plan that Christians have employed often works as follows. First, church members develop natural and mature friendships with those around them—in their neighborhood, on the job, where they shop, and so on. Next, they let their personal lives make an impression upon those whose friendship they cultivate. Everything, naturally, hinges on their personal maturity and Christian commitment. Then, on the basis of an established confidence, they help friends acquire a secure commitment to Jesus Christ.

This type of witnessing has been the church's major asset through the centuries. Presently, we need to refocus it so that it will again bear the major brunt of the church's forward thrust. We are too impatient when the planted seed does not bear fruit immediately. In reality, as in the natural order, the seed must take root and grow at its own rate.

In line with this approach, church leaders today might concentrate on preparing their flocks to develop mature Christian ties with others. Christian lay persons should be freed from the heavy burden of accused dereliction in witness. They also should begin to see that they indeed can and do fulfill their priesthood.

This kind of priestly ministry also extends throughout a Christian's life. Indeed, the opportunities to minister to others are unlimited, if we view the priesthood in proper perspective. Mature Christian lay persons, no less than the pastor, can counsel others. They can hear confessions and remind others of God's forgiveness. They can comfort the bereaved and care for the sick. They can help in all of the *ordinary* ministries of the church and even in the *extraordinary* ones on occasion. Some lay persons have remarkable gifts for helping others, sufficient to alleviate the heavy load carried by their pastors.

In this day of increased specialization, however, we rely upon experts for the doing of extraordinary tasks. Large churches sometimes have the resources to employ specialists who can render more adequate services to the community—that is, beyond the capacities and time of the pastor. Such special ministries might include marriage and family counseling, personal counseling, vocational guidance counseling, legal counseling, financial planning, and others. Resource persons to supply these may often be found within the congregation itself.

To consider only one of these examples, the church has an excellent opportunity to fulfill its priesthood through marriage and family counseling. It ought to assume a major role in this, in fact, for marriage and the family belong to its particular province. A large congregation could employ a person who had specialized training and thus greatly increase the stability of its own membership. He or she could assist them in the turbulent periods of life—marriage, child rearing, divorce, and their attendant crises.

One resource to which the churches should give particular attention in the future is the retired. Besides concerning itself with a ministry to them, it ought also to utilize their training and talents to render many of its priestly ministries. As the retirement age is lowered, a vast reservoir is opened for the churches to tap. Many professional people fall within the ranks of those who could do the church's extraordinary tasks.

Reconcilers Between Persons

Besides its priestly mediation between God and human beings, the church also may mediate Christ's reconciliation between persons. It may assist in breaking down the barriers that exist on account of human sin.

To expect the church to erase all natural distinctions and barriers is too much. It can only strive to bridge as many of the fissures of society as possible. Beginning with the basic units of society, the individual and the family, it might move ever outward in an attempt to make human relations compatible and harmonious. There are a number of serious social gaps that Christians might help transcend.

One is the *age gap*. The turbulent fifties and sixties unveiled the seriousness of this fissure as thousands of youth repudiated the lifestyles and values of their parents and elders. Although all of the churches did not seek direct solutions to the problem, many offered forums for discussion, thus helping to bring improved understanding, which is evident in the seventies. Ideally churches will maintain the atmosphere of an extended family such as Paul envisioned, where older persons are treated as fathers and mothers and younger ones as brothers and sisters (1 Tim. 5:1-2). In this family even slaves and masters would view one another as brothers (1 Tim. 6:2). The churches admittedly fall far short of the ideal at times, but they also do remarkably well at times considering the extent of the age gap.

Another is the *money gap*. Few of us can fail to discern how large and serious the problem of distribution of wealth has become in American society. The crux is, as Clarence Jordan once remarked, "too few people have too much money; too many have too little." Unless our system finds ways to distribute the goods and rewards that it fosters so prolifically, it may not survive. The churches will not play a major role in changing the whole system, perhaps; but with as much wealth as they themselves possess, they can do something. For one thing, they can teach their members some of the early Christian attitudes toward wealth and sharing. Since the early church had few wealthy members, of course, it displayed prejudices toward them that we should not emulate now. However, we can imitate their concern for the poor and their efforts to aid them. Secondly, the churches can set an example of proper stewardship of wealth. This might mean erecting fewer and less costly structures and, instead, investing money in personal causes. Programs might be directed to the elimination of inequality in wealth. Churches might even imitate their early Christian forebears in distributing possessions to the poor.

A third is the *culture gap*. Christianity has a perpetual task of liberating people from their taboos, superstitions, and bugaboos that enslave them to the elements. Society, of course, shares this burden, but the churches cannot relinquish it altogether to the state. The premium placed on education today obligates them more than ever to see that the culturally deprived become well enough equipped to assume their rightful place in society and to develop their potential as creatures of God. Not only so, but the churches will also have to assume a heavy portion of the burden of moral instruction that is breaking down somewhere in the modern educational system. Public schools seem very reluctant to establish definite moral guidelines. Society does not seem able to do it for them. Consequently, the churches remain the most likely instrument for teaching morality.

The churches are already using numerous means for closing the cultural gap. Besides the education that goes on in traditional church programs, they operate preschool and kindergarten programs in impoverished areas, conduct adult education classes in the evenings where the community does not offer such classes, provide scholarships for deserving youth, offer special tutoring services for the handicapped or retarded, purchase books and supplies for those who cannot afford them, and lend their facilities for community educational use. Moreover, they do much to provide incentive for education.

A fourth is the *racial gap*. The churches, just as American society generally, have progressed in this area. Even in the South, it is not unusual to see integrated churches. Nevertheless, true unity of the body of Christ without reference to color is a long way from realization. Christians are still struggling to love one another as *persons*, thus eliminating prejudices directed toward groups. If the churches had solved this problem for themselves, of course, they would be in a position to bandage the wounds of American society. They might hold clinics concerning the establishing of full equality for all in the use of public facilities, for example. They might teach by example that true acceptance goes beyond public laws. Sad to say, some recent incidents make it appear that in the end civic leaders will have to hold clinics for the churches and teach them.

A fifth is the *sex gap*. Concern for women's rights has taken a turn upward in recent years and, unfortunately, has caused a widening rift. With few exceptions American society has handled the issue more deftly than the mainline churches, for the latter, both Protestant and Catholic, find themselves divided into hostile camps over such questions as ordination of women. It is evident that the early churches were not able to act on the principle that in Christ there is "neither male nor female" (Gal. 3:28), but they went beyond either Jewish or Roman society in pursuing the goal. Women such as Lydia, Phoebe, and Priscilla played leading roles in the church. Social strictures alone held them back. The tantalizing question now is whether societal perceptions do not allow the churches actually to implement the principle that, to this point, most have failed to achieve. It is clear that, like the racial fissure, this one will be bridged slowly through much serious effort.

Numerous other gaps could be singled out for comment—some local or regional, some national or international. These five, however, should suffice to illustrate the challenge of the royal priesthood of the faithful. This priestly ministry cannot be fulfilled by a single segment in the church, whether clergy or laity. It belongs to the entire people of God, and it will require their united effort.

10
The Servant Church

In the past century the most heatedly debated aspect of the church's mission is that which emerges from the servant motif. This has not always been true. Early Christianity earned a glossy reputation for its charities and social aid. The Emperor Julian, erstwhile enemy of anything Christian, paid it the highest compliment in imitating these institutions as a part of his effort to revive paganism. "For it is disgraceful," he wrote his high priest in Galatia, "that, when no Jew ever has to beg, and the impious Galilaeans (Christians) support not only their own poor but ours as well, all men see that our people lack aid from us." [1] Julian could have added that Christian inventiveness produced hundreds of institutions to care for the needy, the sick, travelers, widows, orphans, prisoners, the unemployed, victims of calamities, or people having needs of any kind. Indeed, early Christianity had done these things so well that the Emperor Constantine placed the charitable concerns of his empire in the hands of the churches. As a result, the latter fell heir to the same task for many centuries in most nations of Europe.

This same situation still was present in the early American colonies. Most persons looked to the churches for charity and social aid. A significant shift occurred, however, as a by-product of the struggle to obtain and secure religious liberty by way of the separation of church and state. From Roger Williams on, Americans have grown in the conviction that the state holds responsibility for the physical welfare of its citizens, the churches for their spiritual welfare.

Groups such as Baptists, who had so much to gain by the separation of church from state, etched this outlook deeply into their consciences. The result is that they have allowed themselves to tiptoe into social concern only with the most extreme caution. Accordingly, many Protestant groups vigorously opposed the so-called "social gospel movement," which developed in the late nineteenth and early twentieth centuries. "The business of the churches is spiritual, to 'save souls.' The church should not become involved in matters that properly belong to the province of the state." To be sure, opponents made justifiable criticisms of the facile optimism of exponents of a social gospel. But the true roots of their opposition lay in their history.

In the sixties the churches responded in a different way to this issue out of newly awakened sensitivity to massive social crises, not merely in the United States but in the entire world. Even conservative and evangelical groups who had rejected the social gospel movement emphatically now became seriously concerned about and involved in social service, if not social action. Some conservative groups still debate the propriety of social involvement and posit a dichotomy between evangelism and social ministry, but their numbers are diminishing steadily. Among Southern Baptists, for example, both churches and agencies pursue both, having worked out a more or less satisfactory justification for them.

One serious issue that still hangs on, however, is the propriety of social action. Many would say, "Social service, yes! Social action, no!" Before looking at ways in which the churches may discharge the servant role, therefore, we ought briefly to examine this question.

Social Action: Whether, How, and Where?

It is not as easy to establish a basis for social action from New Testament writings as it is to establish one for social service. There can be little question that Jesus and his early followers met human need wherever or in whatever form they found it. As the commission to the twelve (Matt. 10:8) expressed it, they healed the sick, raised the dead, cleansed lepers, cast out demons. There is little to indicate, however, that either Jesus or his early followers organized their efforts to overcome the major social ills. Those first believers preached against such things, it is true. But they left little evidence of acting to eliminate such abuses as slavery, inequality of women, maltreatment of prisoners, war, brutality, poverty, and many others. Quite on the contrary, Paul counseled slaves to accept their situation and to obey their masters (1 Cor. 7:21-22; Eph. 6:5-8; Col. 3:22; Philem. 16), a procedure that must have rankled many slaves who heard him preach that Christ means freedom. It was a long time before Christians and churches sought actively to modify social institutions and customs by direct action.

Whether?

Does this mean, then, that we, too, should avoid social action? Before answering affirmatively, I think we should consider several factors that kept the first Christians from it. One was their expectation of Jesus' imminent return. At one point Paul believed this would happen before his generation died (1 Cor. 15:51), a conviction which necessarily discouraged efforts to change society.

Another was the fact that they were an insignificant minority. What could a small handful of people do to change customs that millions accepted? They would only be rebuffed, ridiculed, or censured for their effort. Before very long, as a matter of fact, they had to worry about surviving. The most they could do was to bear witness to their convictions in quiet ways.

A third was the fact that they belonged mostly to the lower class. As Paul reminded the Corinthians, not many were educated, powerful, or wealthy (1 Cor. 1:26). People of limited education and social station seldom organize to express their grievances. They depend on persons who are better educated to lead them when they do. A fourth was that they were preoccupied with getting another job done within a short time; they could not do other things at the same time.

At the same time we must observe that, as Christianity incorporated persons of wealth and education by the end of the second century, it began to exert its influence for social change. By the time of Constantine, for example, one may discern Christian influence upon imperial legislation. After Constantine, when persecution had abated permanently, Christians played a major role in the transformation of society. Not all of their efforts, perhaps, were commendable. The less commendable side of it was that they gradually proscribed all competitors and made intolerance a public virtue, even persecuting one another with a vengeance. But this development should not cause us to overlook the genuine social contribution their concerted action made—raising the status of women and children, discouraging slavery, generating more humane treatment of prisoners, changing economic values, caring for the sick and needy, and shaping many public customs. As a proportionately large and influential segment of society, they perceived their responsibility differently than they had as a small and inconsequential one.

In the United States the separation of church and state guarantees that no single religious groups will dominate public action as Christians eventually did in the Roman Empire. Indeed, the ability of any religious group to affect public policy, morality, or customs will depend on effective marshalling of opinion or action on a voluntary basis. Even in this kind of arrangement there are dangers.

One is that a large denomination, such as the Roman Catholic Church or the Southern Baptist Convention, may exercise a disproportionate influence, particularly in areas where it embraces the majority of the population. In actual practice, this seldom creates a problem because of internal pluralism of large denominations. Though the Catholic hierarchy could once sway a vote on certain issues—for example, dissemination of birth-control information in Massachusetts—they can hardly do so any more. Baptists have seldom possessed such well-defined and coordinated views that they could implement a policy decision even in a local community. A vote prohibiting sale of alcoholic beverages in some rural county would be more the exception than the rule.

Some risks aside, most religious groups engage in some kind of political action. Much of their real influence would be indirect, through individual constituents. Increasingly, however, it is direct and organized, through agencies and programs designed to influence public policy, such as by lobbying at the local, state, or national levels. Sometimes religious groups act alone, sometimes in concert with others. Several Baptist denominations, as one illustration, lobby in Washington through the Baptist Joint Committee on Public Affairs. Numerous denominations participate in social action programs through local councils and the National Council of Churches.

Essentially, social action programs are a part of the churches' prophetic task. Once prophetic words could be issued effectively by individuals. In the complex urban setting of today, that has become more and more difficult. Effective action depends increasingly upon mutual organized effort. Accordingly, the most distinct prophetic voices today are probably voices of organizations such as Common Cause, Ralph Nader Associates, the NAACP, and others like them. It is not surprising, then, to find churches organizing for social action. By this date most of them will not ask whether they should engage in social action but where and how.

How?

The answer to the first question is: at those places in society where Christian perceptions need to be applied in order to correct injustices, evils, and abuses. The answer to the second, is: in ways which will not conflict with fundamental Christian principles concerning the person and society. Since our approach may have much to do with the issues we take up, it will be useful to consider this matter more fully before giving examples of where we may act.

The focal Christian norm for ethical decisions, *agape* love, would decree, I think, that *we always place persons above causes*. This is not to say that there are no worthy causes for which a person or persons might even give his or her life. But there is seemingly a growing tendency to forfeit the lives of persons for the "worthy cause." From that point it is possible for some to justify acts of terror, guerrilla warfare, and wanton destruction of human life. The argument is: "This cause will aid persons—not those destroyed, but others. The number who give their lives will be smaller than the number helped."

This argument may well be true, but I do not think it will stand up under scrutiny of the fundamental Christian regard for the measureless value of each particular person. If the heavenly Father numbers the hairs of each head, then how much value does he place on each life? Down deep, I think, the approach reflects a basic lack of trust in divine providence. Whatever happens, *we* have to do it; otherwise, it will not get done.

Granted, human effort is important. Many things would not get done if we did not accept responsibility for them. But is it not arrogance which prompts us to suppose that we, finite human beings, will determine the ultimate course of history by acts of limited scope? How can we be so sure that the squandering of human lives and the destruction of the moment will turn out the way we expect? Ought we not rather to subordinate our cause to a deep concern for persons, trusting that "for those who love God, he works all things together for good" (Rom. 8:28, author's translation) or brings them toward some satisfactory conclusion? History proves repeatedly that changes, whether mild or radical, do not always usher in something more amenable to human life than what already existed.

As a Christian, therefore, I would always subordinate causes to persons and entertain modest hopes for the outcome, knowing that under the searchlight of eternity what we are doing may not make as much difference as we think and dream. A person-oriented approach would suggest, secondly, that *we avoid violence in every way possible.* This is not to say that we should avoid doing anything that entails a *risk* of violence. If we followed that rationale, we would be immobilized altogether, for there are few prophetic endeavors which will escape reactions that may sometimes become violent. Rather, Christian concern for persons would encourage the employment only of nonviolent means to obtain changes; it would discourage the use of violence even as a last resort. Willingness to wait upon God is fundamental to our approach to change.

What is suggested by all of this is the grading of our approach into several steps, as suggested in Matthew 18:15-17, concerning disciplinary problems. A first step would be to complain individually or as groups to the parties responsible. If this gained no satisfaction, the next step would be to do everything possible to effect changes through channels established by our political structures. Here patience is extremely important. In the United States the democratic process seems to creak along slowly, but it does work, as the Watergate trials demonstrate.

If, after a protracted effort through established channels, we cannot obtain the desired remedy, then the third step would be to organize protests or demonstrations. Demonstrations have become part and parcel of American political life, fostered, I think, by the fact that it often takes dramatic organized efforts to get the attention of bureaucrats. Such demonstrations are risky, and many of them have gotten out of control. But the orderly and nonviolent protests organized by Martin Luther King, Jr. to obtain civil rights prove that demonstrations can be peaceful. One thing that the marches caution us about, however, is that those who protest must be willing to pay the price of civil disobedience, even when laws are unjust. Otherwise violence will result.

John Woolman, a Quaker of pre-Revolutionary War days, left an example of prophetic witness that is worthy of emulation even today. He was what I would call "a quiet revolutionary." As the conviction grew within him that slaveholding was wrong, Woolman began where he was. First, after his one conscience-searing experience, he personally refused ever again to write a bill of sale for a slave. Then, limiting his own business in order to follow God's leading, he went where he knew he would get some hearing—to Quaker meetings. When invited, he placed before others the burden of his heart.

If he lodged in homes where there were slaves, in the morning he would leave money for his board, unwilling to take advantage of an enslaved brother or sister and intent on leaving an unmistakably clear message. He wore unbleached muslin suits because dye for coloring men's suits was made from indigo, a product of slave labor. In all of this Woolman had little assurance that he would succeed; but he continued, patiently trusting God to use his endeavors. Largely as a result of his efforts, no American Quaker owned a slave after 1787.

Where?

This brief discussion is not intended to serve as a complete guide for social action, but to suggest general guidelines. In what areas might such principles be applied?

An actual example of successful concerted action is the cleanup of Newport, Kentucky, several years ago. Teeming with gamblers, prostitutes, and a crime syndicate, the city appeared to have no prospect of change until church leaders of the city organized a campaign to elect a reform-minded sheriff and drive out the illicit businesses. In this case a solution came through established political processes, but it would never have occurred had concerned Christian citizens not organized their efforts.

Besides this type of local effort, in the fifties and sixties we witnessed many organized marches, demonstrations, and boycotts designed to obtain equal rights for minority groups, to protest United States involvement in the Vietnam war, to gain more favorable working conditions for farm laborers, to call attention to the plight of the poor, to rally support for women's rights, and to draw attention to myriad other causes. None of these efforts was in itself strictly Christian, but millions of Christians, churches, and church leaders participated. In some instances Christians did take leading roles through civil rights organizations such as the Southern Christian Leadership Conference of Martin Luther King, Jr. Many individual causes, of course, will remain controverted by Christians as well as others on account of the pluralism of the church and the nature of the issues themselves, but such involvement is vital to the infusion of Christian perspectives into the American social setting.

Ideally, of course, all of us would like our assessment of issues on which we acted in concert to be unambiguous and unequivocal; but consensus is too much to expect. Not all Christians have supported antiliquor campaigns in a local area, for not all agree on degrees of temperance. Similarly, not all will unite in support of or opposition to sale of pornographic literature, gay rights, abortion, capital punishment, distribution of information about contraceptives or family planning, school textbooks teaching evolution theories, tighter control of handgun sales, busing of school children, open housing, building of nuclear power plants, sale and manufacture of nuclear weapons, and dozens of other issues about which many have deep feelings, for they do not agree on what Christian perceptions require. In some cases they simply cancel one another's efforts. In the end this will mean that individuals and groups will act out of strongly held convictions, trusting that God may use even contradictory efforts in some way to effect his purpose for humanity.

Social Service

Social service is much less disputable than social action. Not only is there unambiguous evidence for it in Jesus' teaching; but Christianity, in all of its diversity, has compiled a commendable record of service, marred only in rare instances by preoccupation with other churchly concerns. Contrary to popular impressions, groups classified as pietistic have shared this record. Admittedly, some evangelical and pietistic groups have spoken out forcefully against the social gospel. Others, however, including the founders of German Pietism in the seventeenth century, have distinguished themselves by social ministries—homes for orphans, schools, alms houses, hospitals, hostels, and prison ministries.

The most remarkable record of social service compiled by any religious group is that of Quakers, whose consistent efforts on behalf of peace, humane treatment of prisoners, the poor, victims of calamity, and other causes are astounding. A study of social service in the United Church of Christ, moreover, revealed that, in that socially oriented denomination, those classified as pietists did the most for others.[2] Rationalists had good perceptions, but they did not act on them as effectively as pietists—confirmation, surely, that spirituality supplies a critical factor in service: motivation.

Making Choices

In the matter of meeting human need wherever we find it, however, there is a severe problem of limited resources. Christianity no longer holds the enviable position it held in Constantine's day, when imperial largesse repeatedly filled the coffers in support of charities and social aid. Yet in America its status is not quite that of pre-Constantinian Christianity, which depended wholly upon the voluntary generosity of members to supply what is needed. There is a cooperative church-state relationship. But no matter how much is given, it will not be enough. The churches will have to make difficult choices about where they expend their efforts. Human needs, even in a nation as affluent as the United States, are so great that choices will have to be carefully made. By what criteria will the churches make these choices? Without claiming to exhaust the possibilities, I would suggest three:

1. *Determine priorities according to need.* Where other institutions—for example, the federal, state, and local government—assume the burden, the churches can relinquish responsibility and allow these to assume it in order to concentrate their resources on areas of greater need. Undoubtedly, their decisions will be influenced by whether

or not they see an opportunity to render *their* unique ministry, announcing the good news of Christ's reign, which distinguishes the church from all other institutions.

2. *Lead the way into new areas of service.* The servant church should possess a sensitivity to human need that is unmatched by any institution created for purely humanistic reasons. Not only should it share in human suffering and need more empathetically; it should also have the wisdom to get to the underlying roots of them. It should perceive the *real* problems in the illnesses of society and minister to persons accordingly.

In our day, this calls for the churches to be alert for experimentation. They may use their understanding of humanity and society to discover new and genuine solutions to human problems. In the past the churches have designed and inaugurated hospitals, hostels, schools, homes for indigents, and countless other charitable agencies. When society assumed a share of the load, they stepped aside and sought other areas in which they could apply their insights, concern, and zeal to meeting human need.

3. *Serve as a prophetic voice calling attention to human need.* This is necessary in that the churches' resources will never go far enough. From pulpits, through news media, in dialogues, wherever they have opportunity—the churches may quicken the conscience of society with a cry for reform. By the sometimes feeble efforts they put forth themselves in correcting abuses and filling needs, they also may jar society awake.

Church-State Cooperation

In recent years churches in the United States have supplemented and extended their meager efforts at social service through cooperation with local, state, and federal governments. Hospitals, schools, homes for the aging and orphans, and numerous other welfare institutions have obtained substantial grants, which help to achieve objectives of both state and church.

For the most part this kind of church and state cooperation has been wholesome. The courts have kept a watchful eye that the traditional separation of church and state not be violated by state support for religion or by prohibition of the free exercise of it, unless it creates problems for the public welfare. Indeed, this cooperation has worked so well that some religious groups are pressing for a reassessment of the principle of separation. The courts contend, with some justification, that the separation, especially in education, has led to deficiencies in moral training and consequently to a breakdown of public morality. Public educators, they observe, have hesitated to articulate moral principles; and, when they have, they have done so only in the most general and humanistic terms. Much more should be done, therefore, to bring religion into public life—via prayers in schools, reading of the Bible, teaching of Christian values, and other public signs of national religious commitment.

One can appreciate the concern here. However, proponents of this view place too much blame for our present moral crisis on separation of church and state and, in their eagerness to solve a moral problem, look past the dangers in what they propose. The crisis in morality is a product of complex changes in contemporary outlook since the Renaissance. As indicated in an earlier chapter, it is connected with a growth of individual consciousness that has eroded the older authority models. While it is true that religious instruction, since intimately bound up with morality, might help to alleviate the crisis, we must be fully cognizant of the price which might be paid, as in the Roman Empire, for a new church-state alliance. Those who would pay first would be minority groups, whose views would be least likely to get a hearing. Later, all others might pay for an establishment of religion, which would mean an establishment of the faith of the majority.

Recognizing the risks, however, some cooperation is both possible and essential in that no one can draw a line between material and spiritual welfare of people. Questions of legitimacy in dispensing aid to church-related colleges or other institutions should not prevent a search for ways in which the task of caring for the citizens of our society as persons can be effectively discharged.

The Churches and Higher Education

One of the ways in which the churches have served humanity through the centuries is in education. From the early Middle Ages to a century or so ago, in fact, they supplied most of the educational institutions in the West. In the United States, for instance, of 182 permanent colleges established before 1860, 175 were founded by churches. In 1860 there were only seventeen state institutions of higher learning.

Since the Morrill Act of 1862, however, the state has gotten more and more deeply into public higher education and gradually edged the churches out. Today church-supported colleges claim less than 15 percent of the student populace. Most are having serious financial problems. Federal and state governments have stepped in to alleviate these slightly, but the bulk of public monies is still poured into the state-supported schools.

Colleges and universities. In the 1960s I wrote pessimistically about the future of church-supported colleges and universities. It was not that I could see no purpose for them; rather, I doubted whether they could survive. Today I have altered my judgment completely. Their survival is still tenuous from a financial point of view, but it is *essential* from a cultural point of view. One can only hope that the public will find ways to help these institutions to survive, perhaps by way of direct tuition grants to needy students rather than direct aid to the schools. Other types of aid appear more questionable inasmuch as, even when legal, they introduce so much governmental regulation as to thwart the purposes of church-supported colleges.

The fact is, we are now confronted with an educational crisis in western civilization. This crisis is related to the cultivation of the powers of empirical observation and rational analysis at the expense of what Theodore Roszak has called "the powers of transcendence." The triumph of public higher education has aided and abetted this trend toward "the single vision." For, in the United States especially, institutions of higher learning have seen themselves as service institutions, devoted to meeting the demands of the public. And what the public has demanded has been more and more science and technology to raise the standard of living, create more and better conveniences, and solve problems externally. It is highly significant of this trend that, in 1960, federal monies for higher education were distributed 40 percent for defense, 37 percent for medical research, 20 percent for other sciences, and 3 percent for social sciences, but nothing for humanities. Even if this distribution has changed since, it has not changed dramatically and cannot be expected to do so.

If there is to be a significant shift in approaches to education, a recovery of some balance between empirical/rational and intuitive powers, it will have to come from the church-related schools. Whether they can do anything, moreover, will depend to a great degree upon how clearly they define their purposes in *contradistinction* to and not in agreement with the purposes of state-supported schools. The latter necessarily define their purposes in relationship to the *state*. The former must define their purposes in relationship to the *church*. From this point of view church-related colleges would have two purposes: (1) to offer models of education properly balanced between empirical/rational and intuitive, and (2) to send a stream of graduates into all the vocations of western society, equipped to make an impact on the direction of the society. For both purposes quality education is essential.

In regard to modeling, church-supported colleges can hardly avoid training men and women for the same vocations for which other institutions of higher learning prepare them. However, they can avoid that specialism that is an underlying cause of the breakdown of western civilization by offering an integrated concept of life, one that brings God into the picture as the Creator and sustainer of human life, who is "in all, through all, and above all things."

Church-supported colleges will of necessity have to think of their influence on culture in terms of salt and light. The focus should be on persons whose perceptions have been shaped by a core of humanistic cultural studies in which religion was the integrating factor. The goal ought to be the formation of persons who will respond as persons to their environment, to other persons, and to the Ultimate. Such formation should take place within community, something almost entirely absent from large and complex universities of the United States. The churches alone probably stand ready, in smaller colleges and universities, to form communities where authentic personal formation can occur. It is out of community that students will develop openness, trust, warmth, and compassion for other persons and for their world.[3]

Campus ministries. Without minimizing the contribution church-related colleges and universities can make to the churches' mission, we must acknowledge that 85 percent of the students in the United States go to public-supported schools. It follows from this that a large proportion even of the churches' as well as the society's future leaders will be trained there. Secondly, if the churches wish to have a continuing impact on the culture of tomorrow, they must expand their ministry to the campuses across the nation. Currently they invest far too little in this crucial ministry.

From the point of view of the churches' mission, the picture is somewhat cloudy. On the one hand, religion is popular among students. Where courses in religion are offered, they attract hundreds— mostly students who have fairly strong ties with the churches already. After many years of debate, moreover, there is general agreement that religion belongs in the college curriculum, so that the demand for courses is being met.

On the other hand, the churches do not have input into what is taught and who teaches. Separation of church and state requires that religion courses be taught not merely from a nonsectarian point of view but as a cultural study. Although this approach assures that students will get exposure to the elements of religion, it does not assure that they will get a sympathetic presentation of their own faith. Quite often, as a matter of fact, university courses in religion will run directly counter to what students have learned in their earlier religious training at home or at church. This is not to criticize university professors, although some cannot claim lack of bias in their attitude toward the churches, but to point up the dilemma the churches confront. The experience of religious instruction on the campus can be destructive for the student unless we find ways to bridge the gap between campus and church. Several avenues now appear open.

1. One is sometimes offered by the college or university itself. Many individual professors and departments of religion in state-supported schools are sympathetic and cooperative with the churches. Legally, of course, they must walk a tightrope. As teachers, they cannot speak for the churches. As individuals, however, they can bear witness to their own faith in ways not touching the teaching-learning process.

2. Another is chairs of religion supported by churches but accredited by the state-supported college or university. Such chairs probably have a tenuous future as religion becomes more and more a part of the college curriculum. At the moment, however, many schools that do not have departments of religion grant credit for classes taught by approved instructors. The instructors, since not directly paid by the state-supported school, may exercise a certain degree of freedom university professors cannot. The churches should respond, therefore, to opportunities to teach religion in this way; but they should not be optimistic for the long run.

3. A third, and probably the most viable, is campus ministry supported by the churches directly. Most state-supported schools will employ a chaplain or other persons to assist students with personal problems. As in the teaching process, however, such persons usually maintain a certain amount of detachment from the churches. Church-sponsored campus ministry, therefore, provides the best bridge from church to campus.

Unfortunately, many churches do not allow campus ministers sufficient freedom to develop and implement programs suitable for the campus. It is understandable that they wish to keep such programs anchored firmly to local church programs. But this fails sufficiently to discern the unusual situation of the student during his or her college days. By design a university is out on the forefront of society—a generation ahead, as it were. This means that students are experiencing and learning things that make them uncomfortable in traditional church setting. For many, church can be experienced only in the intimate setting of a student religious fellowship. As long as they maintain loose ties with local congregations, they will usually make a reentry by the time they are ready to leave college. To give this kind of freedom for campus ministries to be the church on campus requires a measure of faith, but it is one that will usually be repaid.

4. A fourth, not to be neglected, avenue is the ministry of local congregations to college youth. Many churches have special classes and activities for collegians. One important aspect of this ministry is cognitive, helping students integrate faith and what they are learning on campus. Another is affective, helping them to cope with

the passage from childhood to young adulthood with all the attendant stresses involved.

Conclusion. Both church-supported colleges and ministries to the campus form an important facet of the churches' servant ministry. They involve a huge act of faith, for their consequences are not immediately visible. Whether or not we have invested wisely will be more visible tomorrow than today. But we cannot afford not to take the risk.

The Churches and Healing/Helping Ministries

Another area in which the churches have served humanity is that of healing or helping. Many will be surprised to learn that the chief contribution of Christianity in this regard may be in the development of institutions such as hospitals and orphans' homes. The ancient world, for instance, did not lack charities and social aid; what it lacked was organized charities and social aid that would care for all persons impartially and without expectation of return. Too much of the Roman largesse, like Americans, aided those who least needed it, those who could repay in kind. Christianity came along to offer aid to the totally dependent.

Hospitals. At present a shift is occurring in areas of need, and the churches need to think about shifting their focus of ministry as well. At one time society manifested little interest in hospital care, and the churches stepped in to build and operate the first hospitals. Presently public interest in providing proper medical care for all citizens has resulted in national programs of Medicare and Medicaid. These programs pay for care in either private or public facilities, so that few persons go without proper help. Church-supported hospitals, as a result, now operate essentially as private hospitals. They charge prices comparable to private, profit-making institutions. They care for charity patients only where churches pay for their care, so that they no longer fall into the category of charitable institutions. If the churches continue to maintain control over them, they will do so only out of concern for the added religious flavor that they may give through chaplains or others.

Care of the aging. Meantime, our society has not awakened fully to some other areas of pressing need in healing and helping. One

example is care of the aging. True, most states operate homes for
the aging; and there are many private facilities now where social
security benefits and medical programs pay for such services. Recent
reports on both public and private homes for the aging, however,
reveal a painful lack of sensitivity and actual help for the burgeoning
number of older persons. The fault rests partly with families of the
aging, who put them out of sight and out of mind. But it also rests
with the institutions. The elderly are often poorly fed and improperly
cared for in times of illness, which are frequent. They grow lonely
out of lack of contact with others. Handicapped by poor eyesight,
hearing, and health, they withdraw into a self-imposed seclusion
until they die.

The churches can respond to this area of need in several ways.
The place to begin may be by teaching their members to assume
responsibility to look after their grandparents and parents, as early
Christians did (1 Tim. 5:4). We recognize, of course, that our social
customs have changed here. Having moved from a rural to an urban
society, we no longer maintain those nuclear family units that included several generations. Thus all of us have become more dependent upon individual or governmental care. But, in our day, is there
not still a place for genuine familial concern? How much might
this help to alleviate loneliness for the aging? Having said that,
however, most of us know that the aging do not want to burden
their families and cannot always be properly cared for by them.

Consequently, in the second place, the churches should consider
the erection and maintenance of additional homes for the aging that
will exemplify Christian sensitivity. Obviously, they will lack resources to operate all the facilities which might be needed; but they
can model authentic Christian care in such a way that they will
influence what happens in other institutions.

In the third place, they can maintain active ministries to the aging
in public and private homes that already exist, as many churches
do now. This would include assisting elderly persons to find suitable
places, helping them deal with the trauma of moving, visiting them
regularly while they are there, conducting religious services, taking
them on outings from time to time, bringing them articles that they
need, and assisting them to cope during their twilight time.

Multiservice centers. During the sixties churches increasingly moved in the direction of developing centers that would provide multiple services to the needy. Sometimes individual churches, sometimes denominational agencies, sometimes ecumenical groups operate these. They include an endless variety of services: medical and dental clinics, legal aid and counsel, day care for working mothers, mothers' day out child care, Head Start tutoring, financial aid, family counseling, arts and crafts, food baskets, and many others. In many cases such programs will be partially funded by government grants.

Halfway houses. An interesting extension of the servant ministry of the church is halfway houses of one type or another. Among the most widely known of these was Dismas House in Saint Louis, Missouri, which served as a reentry center for convicts. It gave them a place to stay until they found jobs and helped them to get located within society again. Variations on this plan are Emmaus House, a facility for transient and homeless women, and Augusta House, a refuge for alcoholic women. The former is aimed at helping women through temporary crisis situations, the latter at longer-term rehabilitation. Augusta House, recently opened in Louisville, Kentucky, receives seventy dollars a month per resident from the Metropolitan Social Services Department. The rest of its support depends on church contributions. Similar houses assist drug users, delinquents, and others in the rehabilitation process.

Such facilities as these obviously entail heavy risks, and they often close as a result of criticism. Their aims, however, coincide well with the attitude Jesus himself manifested toward the people of his day who could not cope.

Areas of Pressing Need

Before closing this discussion of the servant ministry, it will be appropriate to call attention to some examples of urgent new social problems that demand the attention of the churches and the application of Christian perceptions.

World hunger. Economists already are talking of applying the battlefield principle of triage, dividing the hungry into three groups—those who will starve anyway, those who have a strong chance of survival, and those who have a fifty-fifty chance. Some say we should forget the first group and concentrate on the second and as many of the third as seems feasible. I do not believe the churches can opt for this crass solution. Above all, we must not allow ourselves to be put off by the seeming hopelessness of the situation. We have to trust God to use whatever efforts we expend to deal with the crisis. We can learn from people like John Woolman to begin where we are, to work at the problem where we are part of the problem.

Keeping this in mind, the churches can do something significant: (1) They can help their own constituency to realize that, despite our removal from it, there is a world hunger crisis. More than education is needed, however. Most Christians need first to be conscientized by making the hungry objects of prayer. From this may come action to alleviate hunger. (2) They can teach the biblical concept of contentment (Phil 4:10-14; Matt. 6:25-34). Indeed, it might be an appropriate time to reconsider whether we could not emulate the early Christians in fasting two days a week, not depriving ourselves of all food but cutting our intake. Our end of the problem involves overconsumption and waste. (3) They can collect money and possibly even food for distribution. In Louisville an organization called Louisville United Against Hunger, sponsored by all denominations, spends every dime sent to feed the poor—half in the United States and half abroad. Administrative costs for this organization are borne by one of the churches.

The energy crunch. The churches might offer similar service with reference to the energy crisis that has made itself so evident in the past few years. (1) They can furnish an example to their members in wise use of energy. Old buildings, when remodeled, could be designed to conserve energy. New ones could be built with conservation a primary aim. (2) Church leaders can set an example for others in energy saving. For instance, they could conserve gasoline by walking, riding bicycles, using public transportation, driving smaller cars, pooling rides, or planning travel more carefully. (3) The churches could develop instructional programs in energy use. The more discussion this topic gets, the more likely people will become sensitive. (4) Most important of all, they can cultivate a philosophy of contentment that will militate against maximum consumption and waste, which is so prevalent in American society.

Child abuse. The growth of child abuse mentioned earlier is another serious social issue that demands the attention of the churches. They might act in several ways to get at not merely the problem of abuse but its underlying causes. (1) They can inculcate those Christian virtues love and patience, which stand over against the anger and hotheadedness that lead to child abuse. (2) They can work to eliminate some of the social pressures and perspectives that generate frustration and anger. Perhaps here we are talking about what Toffler has called "future shock." If nothing else, religious groups can slow the pace of change and provide sanctuaries for making more gradual transitions. (3) They can maintain vigilance about cases of child abuse or neglect and, when they discover them, work with authorities to prevent further abuse.

Theft, vandalism, mugging of elderly or handicapped persons. Recent newspaper reports have called attention to an increase of acts of terrorism against elderly persons in large cities such as Oakland, Philadelphia, New York, and Chicago. Law enforcement is obviously a police problem, and in the long run large urban complexes will have to give way to new social structures. Sociological studies show that crimes of this type increase where there are unemployment, drug abuse, and inadequate recreational and mental health resources.

However, the churches can do something immediately to lessen the risk and to eliminate causes. (1) Some churches are providing bus service for the elderly or handicapped so that they can shop without being molested. In Philadelphia groups of youths accompanied the elderly personally. (2) Churches also may help to eliminate the causes by sponsoring tutoring programs, assisting in job placement, providing recreational facilities and programs in inner-city areas, and creating other aids to the poor. (3) In Louisville two ministers recently began a program called Christian Youth Alliance, aimed at development of moral character. This program, operating in a deprived and high crime area, provides a central location for job referral information, recreation programs, spiritual guidance, and professional advice. Eventually the designers want to build a youth center that will supply a temporary home as well as these other services for needy youths.

Leisuretime. Few of us could have anticipated the problem use of leisuretime would present. Leisure, of course, is not a problem all experience; but it confronts enough persons, especially the affluent, to deserve mention. The churches may help in several ways. (1) They can sponsor discussions in which people may together reflect on ways to use their leisure more profitably. (2) At the same time they might tap a valuable resource for their own programs. Many professionals will gladly donate some time to minister to needy persons. A medical doctor or dentist, for example, might give some time in a multipurpose center in an impoverished area. A carpenter might assist elderly or handicapped persons in repairing a home. The possibilities are extensive. (3) Churches can also plan recreational activities that will provide a Christian setting for play. Many churches have access to excellent campsites and recreational facilities. In this way there may be opportunities for expanding the educational efforts while meeting a genuine need.

Conclusion

As servant, the church confronts a task far beyond its own resources. It undertakes nothing less than Christ's continuing ministry in and to the world. Because the task is so formidable, we might well become frightened or discouraged and thus beg off from this commission. It is important, therefore, that we have sufficient faith to believe that God will multiply our meager and inadequate efforts. Francis of Assisi is a good model for us to look to here. He wanted nothing more or less than to follow Christ in pouring out his life in service. After renouncing his father's wealth and comfortable life-style he went about caring for lepers, begging to feed the poor, repairing churches that had fallen into a decadent state, and, in short, meeting need wherever he found it. The prayer which bears his name, but which he did not write, encapsules the servant motif that we ought always to embody. It seems especially appropriate to close this chapter with it as our prayer.

> O Lord, Our Christ, may we have thy mind and thy spirit;
> Make us instruments of Thy peace;
> Where there is hatred, let us sow love;

Where there is injury, pardon;
Where there is discord, union;
Where there is doubt, faith;
Where there is despair, hope;
And where there is sadness, joy.

O divine Master, grant that we may not so much seek
To be consoled, as to console;
To be understood, as to understand;
To be loved, as to love;
For it is in giving that we receive,
It is in pardoning that we are pardoned,
And it is in dying that we are born to eternal life.

Amen!

11
The City of God

The final image whose implications I will attempt to apply to the mission of the church, that of the city of God, is one that may speak most directly to modern civilization since the latter is now essentially urban in character. In some ways it is surprising that, since Christianity began as an urban religion, the modern city has posed such massive problems for the Christian mission. One might have expected better. But it is true, as Johannes C. Hoekendijk[1] remarked, that "when the first stone was laid for the modern industrial cities, the church was absent from the ceremony."

The blame for this state of affairs lies partly in history, partly in the failing of Christians and churches. The historical aspect is complex. By the time Rome fell in the West in A.D. 476, Christianity was no longer essentially urban; it had moved to the countryside. During the so-called "Dark Ages," Europe became agrarian and did not return to an urban economy until about 1200 and after. As it did so, several dramatic events were preparing for a split between church and society.

One was the cultural revolution called the Renaissance, which stressed the authority of the individual and de-emphasized that of the church. Another was the Protestant Reformation, which directly split the church and created two essentially conflicting societies with different sets of values. A third was the so-called Enlightenment of the seventeenth century, which gave birth to the scientific method on which the modern industrialized world has relied so heavily. The cry of the Enlightenment was for a reasonable approach to all matters of life, including religion, and an end to the dogmatism and religious bigotry that produce wars and persecution. A fourth was the industrial revolution of the eighteenth and nineteenth centuries, which finally freed Europe from medieval regulations that had controlled the production and distribution of wealth and substituted competition as the governing principle for modern society. The first landmark of this revolution, Adam Smith's *Wealth of Nations,* appeared in the same year the American colonies published their Declaration of Independence.

What the Industrial Revolution has meant has been a vast leap in the size of cities. To cite only a few examples, whereas the city of Liverpool in England had an estimated 4,000 inhabitants in 1685, and 30,000 to 40,000 in 1760, by 1881 it had 552,425. Whereas the city of Manchester had an estimated 6,000 in 1685, and 28,000 to 45,000 in 1760, by 1881 it had 393,676. Whereas the city of Birmingham had an estimated 4,000 in 1685, and 28,000 to 30,000 in 1760, by 1881 it had 400,757.[2] As late as the early seventeenth century, the city of London, now nearly ten million strong, had no more than 300,000 people.

With this vast leap has come a new attitude—a shift in faith, as it were. Since science and technology, more than any other factor, made urban civilization possible, the faith of the masses has shifted to them. Not divine but human power and genius made these things possible. Thus, where in the Middle Ages people saw the church spire at the center of the village marking the axis around which society turned, heard the bells on the church steeple toll the hours in the day, marked off their calendars with holy days, and turned to the priest for advice, now they look to industry and commerce to set clock and calendar and to the scientist and technician to obtain advice.

It is not entirely the churches' fault, then, that they have never gotten a firm foothold in the cities. But they *are* partially to blame. Until recently, Protestant churches especially have been remiss in trying to minister in the cities. By and large, they did not identify with the working-class plight during the Industrial Revolution. Indeed, it is possible to argue, as Max Weber did, that the Protestant ethic, John Calvin's ethic, produced capitalism, although many scholars now strongly debate the accuracy of this view. In actual fact, however, Protestants did not lend real support to the labor union movement, the social gospel movement, or other efforts to solve the crises created by urbanization.

Roman Catholics have done much better, as religious censuses for the large industrial cities of America will readily prove. In his famous encyclical *Rerum novarum*, issued in 1891, Pope Leo XIII showed his awareness of the plight of the working masses. "But all agree," he wrote, "and there can be no question whatever, that some remedy must be found, and found quickly, for the misery and wretchedness pressing so heavily and unjustly at this moment on the vast majority of the working class." [3] He proceeded to urge Catholics to mediate between labor and capital, contending that "there is no intermediary more powerful than Religion . . . in drawing the rich, and the poor bread-winners, together, by reminding each class of its duties to the other, and especially of the obligations of justice." [4]

He also exhorted the states to step in to alleviate the situation of the oppressed: to pass laws concerning greedy speculation, health and safety, and abuses of women and children in factories. Finally, he lauded those Catholics who had formed associations that would seek to obtain these ends. As a result of aggressive action in this crucial period, Roman Catholics gained a strong constituency in the burgeoning industrial centers as Protestants fled to the suburbs or stayed in the towns and hamlets.

Against such a bleak background as has been painted thus far, it may seem that the concept of the city of God offers little help in trying to frame the mission of the church today. As might be expected, secular theologians of the sixties objected strenuously to its implications, for it seemed to them to be too world renouncing, a relic of the medieval spirit and outlook that is alien to the modern one. It would be better, they thought, to affirm humanity and the earthly city—even to applaud the edging out of God and religion—for this secularization of society simply proves humanity's "coming of age." Human beings have at last reached the stage where they could cope with life entirely on their own.

The Human City

Before exploring more fully the implications of the city of God image for the mission of Christianity, I think it will be useful to assess the latter conclusion at greater length. If we have come of age, as this view supposes, then we may have no mission. If we have yet to reach this state, then we will need to define our mission in relationship to a Christian understanding of humanity.

In the biblical view, the city and the science that brought it about belong to God's purpose in the creation of humanity. God created humanity out of love in order that human beings might have "dominion over the whole earth." [5] The psalmist seemed awestruck by humanity as the summit of God's creative work. "Thou hast made him little less than God,/and dost crown him with glory and honor" (Ps. 8:5). The earth itself and everything in it was placed here for humanity's use.

The city, of course, would represent a vital part of humankind's intended dominion. God did not intend for human beings to be alone. The animals and other living things and, more specifically, other human beings were created to be humanity's helpers (Gen. 2:18 ff.). Fellowship with God implies fellowship with all his creatures. In this respect the biblical view differs from Aristotle's. Where the latter ascribed the existence of a state to the fact that human beings are "by nature" political animals, the biblical writers attributed this to God's purpose. Through fellowship with their Creator human beings find community with one another; together they fulfill the divine purpose—to people the earth and to rule it as their own.

Unfortunately, as things now stand, humanity scarcely approximates, much less matches, the divine purpose. Instead of a universal community of love, there is a veritable tower of Babel. The human community has given way to a mass of cliques and factions, divided and partitioned by a multiplicity of differences. The good creation of God is twisted and distorted and turned to evil and malicious puposes. Genesis 4—11 depicts the situation a bit strongly but does not miss the mark entirely in saying that every imagination of human thoughts "was only evil continually" (Gen. 6:5). Murder, theft, pillage, rape, drunkenness, gluttony, covetousness—the whole lot of vices mar the real character of humanity.

Why? How did this state of affairs develop? According to the dominant biblical view, it resulted from humanity's unwillingness to accept its natural role. Instead of being human, creaturely, human beings sought to be God, the Creator. "Though knowing God," Paul said, "they did not praise or give thanks to him as God, but rather they grew vain in their rationalizations and their uncomprehending heart was darkened" (Rom. 1:21, author's translation).

The human attempt to play God, an unbecoming role, resulted in an unnatural and unsuitable relationship to the creation. Far from having dominion over it, human beings became its slave. They depicted God in the image of birds, animals, reptiles, or even themselves, worshiping the creature rather than the Creator. This perversion produced a perversion in the human being's relationship with himself, for he gave vent to natural appetites to the extent that he too became unnatural, "changed the natural use into that which is against nature" (Rom. 1:26, author's translation). God, of course, according to Paul, allows this to happen. Freedom and the responsibility it entails belong to human nature. The fall, therefore, is humanity's own fault, and human beings are left without an excuse (Rom. 2:1).

Viewing the human situation from this point, we can see that human knowledge and science, though inherently good, become problematic, not in isolation but in connection with human personal character. Human reason, too, suffers distortion in its alienation from the Creator, its autonomy, and its misdirection vis-à-vis the rest of the creation. To state the matter in contemporary idiom, human scientific skills may be applied both to good and evil purposes. At one and the same time they may humanize and dehumanize humanity.

Consider, for example, our advanced mechanical technology. The same science that lightens the burden of human toil and enables human beings to move mountains with push-button controls also fashions weapons of war that can destroy human life with careless abandon. Or consider our medical technology. The same genius that enables science to stay the hand of death in conquering diseases and through organ transplants also has devised gases and germs to be employed in slaughtering whole races.

The city also exhibits the polarities of the human lot. Despite the fact that its provision for community effort has elevated the level of human life to almost unimagined plateaus, the ghettoism that goes with it has plunged masses into unimaginable despair. In the context of their much simpler mode of life, the ancient Greeks used to think of dehumanization as becoming like an animal. In our context we have discovered that dehumanization may descend much lower than the animal level. Human beings may and do lose altogether their personhood when they become a statistic of war or a ghetto problem. When they have lost any sense of purpose and fulfillment in life, as many have, they have ceased to be human. Far better was the lot of the ancient beggar whose cry at the gate could be heard by passersby than that of the multitudes who cannot be heard above the din of the city's massive industry, whirling traffic, and cloud-high buildings.

From a theological perspective the city must be seen as posing the greatest possible threat to humanity's real humanity in that urban life—nay, the whole scientific and technological revolution—tends to undercut human God-consciousness. In the prescientific era in which he lived, Paul could say that "ever since the creation of the world his invisible nature, namely, his eternal power and deity, has been clearly perceived in the things that have been made" (Rom. 1:20). Paul and his contemporaries still lived close to nature. But what about persons in the scientific era who have at best a secondhand contact with nature? What they "clearly perceive," if I may para-phrase Paul, is *human* creative activity, for the metropolis which they know exhibits everywhere the genius of human beings.

I believe that the Jesuit Father Alfred Delp, executed by the Nazis in 1945, conceived and stated the dilemma rightly. A familar theme of his *Prison Mediations* was that "man today is profoundly Godless." Not only so, Delp went on to warn, but "the malady is even more serious; modern man is no longer capable of knowing God." Certain human faculties "have become atrophied and no longer function normally." Moreover, "the structure and constitution of human life today put such a strain on humanity that man is no longer able to express his true nature." [6]

Harmony and peace, instinctive needs of human beings, as Thomas Merton said, are almost wholly absent from our technological society.

> We seek the meaning of our life in activity for its own sake, activity without objective, efficacy without fruit, scientism, the cult of unlimited power, the service of the machine as an end in itself . . . .
> In any event I believe the reason for the inner confusion of Western man is that our technological society has no longer any place in it for wisdom

that seeks truth for its own sake, that seeks the fulness of being, that seeks
to rest in an intuition of the very ground of all being.[7]

Many persons will confirm Merton's judgment today.

When we undertake to analyze this situation in theological perspective, we might say that the basic human problem has not changed
its essential character. What has changed is the *magnitude* of the
problem. How can human beings, immersed in an impersonal and
artificial world, find themselves and their community with their own
kind in the true source of their existence? Can they bring God into
the picture of human life and particularly into the picture of each
person's existence? Somehow theological reflections must answer
these questions. And in this respect our task has one more step than
Paul's. For where Paul had to show persons who already believed
in the spiritual how to believe rightly, we have to show them how
to believe in the spiritual; only then can we tell them how to believe
rightly.

The City of God and the City of Man

At this point we may return to consideration of the concept of
the city of God in its implications for the urban mission. As articulated
by Augustine in his classic work, this concept speaks directly to
our present task.

On the one hand, it reminds us that it is pure folly to think that
this city will be fully realized here and now. It did not happen
with Constantine. It will not happen in any western or Marxist
utopian society. As long as human beings live, there will be a mixture
of selflessness and selfishness. Human institutions, even the church,
will fail to achieve the ideal. Whatever it is we aspire to, we must
temper our aspirations with a realistic assessment of our human
limitations and, above all, our tendency to turn what is good to
evil and destructive purposes.

On the other hand, the idea also reminds us of the possibilities
of the church to build its aspirations and hopes upon what God
is doing in and for humanity. No society can long survive the process
of depersonalization, despiritualization, and dehumanization that has
overtaken western civilization. Christianity, representing roughly a

third of the total population of the world, offers a real hope for altering this process, already very evident, before it is too late. As Christians, we must be quite clear about our stance with references to the so-called secularization, and the idea of the city of God offers at least one point on the compass for doing so.

As the writer of the *Letter to Diognetus* would have expressed it had he lived in our day, Christians may by no means oppose *eo ipso* the scientific and technological revolution that is building the metropolis. To whatever extent this revolution humanizes persons, they may applaud what is taking place. The improvement of the human estate through provision of food, clothing, housing, recreation, medicine, and the rest represents in a significant way the divine purpose for humanity. As citizens of the human city, Christians will contribute their share to the building of a stable and wholesome society. As always, they will be good citizens, by prayer, word, and deed helping to construct a sound fabric in the body politic. They will share the manner of the life characteristic of their time, although being critical of it, and be obedient of the established laws insofar as these contribute genuinely to the welfare of human beings.

This positive attitude toward the human city in no way implies a blanket approval, as some secularizers would have it. The fundamental antipathy between the city of God and the human city exists still wherever depersonalization, despiritualization, and dehumanization occur in the secular city. As long as these continue, the church has an urgent mission to the human city.

A Heavenly Citizenry

The first task of the pilgrim people who make up the church is to fashion a heavenly citizenry who can show forth the true end and purpose of humanity. Since this concern has already been articulated in connection with our discussion of the image of the new humanity, it will suffice to underline here the importance of a nucleus committed unequivocally to the mission task.

The most obvious fact about the churches' situation in the metropolises and cosmopolises of today is that they find themselves relegated to increasingly inconspicuous places. Persons accustomed to thinking of the church in its rural and small-town setting as one of the dominant institutions in society may find this discovery unsettling and even distressing. Before we join the chorus of those ready to write Christianity's epitaph, however, let us remember that we now have far more reason for optimism than Christians of the first three centuries and possibly even any other generation. Our passage from Christendom to a post-Christian era and from a rural to an urban setting simply means that we cannot rely on public pressure to assist the mission.

In such a setting we are driven back once more to the truth of Paul's observation about our source of confidence in Christian mission. It is not in ourselves, in our own resources. The task is too immense. Our personal resources are too small. "Rather, our adequacy (for this mission task) is from God, who *made* us adequate to be ministers of a new covenant" (2 Cor. 3:5-6, author's paraphrase).

Stated another way, our citizenship in the city of God is not automatic. It is a gift. We have been naturalized, as it were, by way of adoption into God's family. The Spirit produces from the human city the citizens of the city of God. He calls them to faith and discipleship. He sets them apart for service to God and to other persons. He instills the virtues of "love, joy, peace, patience, kindness, goodness, faithfulness, gentleness, self-control" (Gal. 5:22-23). He provides an assurance of the final hope of humanity.

If Christian citizenship is a gift, then our part will be to prepare to receive it. We place ourselves at God's disposal, as it were, not expecting particular things to happen but waiting expectantly upon him in prayer and worship. We seek awareness of his presence in and through our experience of life. We beg of him a vision of his purpose within the maze of conflicting events that surround us. Withdrawal from the hubbub of the human city to pray and worship are necessities, not luxuries, for living a fully human life in a tangled world.

Salt and Light and Soul

Within the human city, Christians may fill the functions of "salt" and "light" (Matt. 5:13-14) or, as the *Epistle to Diognetus* phrased it, "soul" for the world. Wherever they are, whatever they are doing, they let their light shine so that through their good character and deeds, other persons may recognize the presence and action of God (Matt. 5:16).

All three images are especially fitting today in that they presuppose a minority situation for the churches. The minority have the task of salting and lighting and vivifying the world. Specifically with reference to the urban mission, this suggests that we help people individually and corporately to perceive a hidden dimension, the transcendent dimension, which makes human life whole. Though persons may live independently of God, or at least of an open acknowledgment of him, we believe they cannot be whole persons without God. Both by involving persons in the fellowship we experience in the gathering of communities and by our mission activity, we seek to awaken them to the reality of God and, through this awakening, to the fullness of human life.

This conception of our missionary task may involve considerable adjustment in the way we have tended to envision missions heretofore. For one thing, we might replace a decided negativism with a more positive understanding of humanity and its plight. Our Puritan heritage in American Protestantism has caused us to lay heavy emphasis upon human unworthiness, hopelessness, and irreformability. There has even been a negative attitude toward the enjoyment of life; true discipleship has been depicted as a kind of flight from a dreary world. Now in a remarkably demanding era, where the physical possibilities of enjoying life have bloomed so vividly, many persons refuse or perhaps are unable to take such thought seriously. They are not prepared to hear a dirge played in the midst of their celebration of life's gifts.

On the other side, this negativism tends to overload a frame already straining from the demands placed upon it by complex urban society. A Harvard psychologist pointed out a few years ago that 15 percent of all Americans born after 1985 will be unable to cope—that is, in terms of the complexities of the society, they will be mentally retarded. The emotional demands of this intricate way of life siphon off all human resources. The sense of insufficiency and inadequacy is immense.

For such persons, therefore, a prime task of the churches is to help them tap into resources that many have not yet discovered. In fine, this means to direct them to the one thing or rather the One who is needful for life. This presupposes, of course, that the churches will have discovered that reality for themselves. If they have not, how will they direct others to it? From a practical standpoint, this mission may be effected through several channels.

One is conversion of life and character. At various times in recent years both Christians and non-Christians have questioned efforts at conversion. In some ways their skepticism was justifiable. For one, bogus and superficial conversions have occurred, involving little real change of character. Indeed, throughout Christian history Elmer Gantry-type characters have preyed on gullible believers for personal profit to their shame. For another, conversion accounts frequently fit into stereotypes that leave their content open to dispute. For another, even devout converts show lack of discrimination regarding what is genuinely Christian and what is cultural veneer.

Conceding all of these things, I would still argue both the need and the possibility of conversion. As is true of numerous other ideas or practices, what conversion means requires fuller consideration. It has often been understood in static terms as abandonment of certain universally acknowledged vices and adoption of equally well-fixed virtues. Human life, however, is never so static that conversion can be defined in this way. Rather, in the Christian view it entails an inward transformation, a change of heart, which will produce a wholly new attitude of personal responsibility toward God, oneself, other persons, and the world. This understanding of conversion admittedly leaves us a complex problem of working out relationships from the inside out. But there can be little doubt that, for many, Christ truly makes all things new (2 Cor. 5:17).

A second channel for effecting this mission is *Christian presence.* It is precisely this which the metaphors of salt, light, and soul suggest about the mission of the church. To what extent or how Christians differ from other persons will remain always hidden. There is, nonetheless, an element of this hidden life which may manifest itself through the external fabric of life—character, words, and deeds. In homes, shops, stores, factories, fields, schools, stadiums—wherever the church scatters or gathers—the life of Christ within us, the confessedly strange character of our heavenly citizenship, may penetrate the life of every day. In essence we are talking here about faith and hope and love and all those other characteristics that together display the new life in Christ. Again, I ask, is anything so critical as opening the doors of our hearts and minds to let divine love flow in to create and shape these traits in us?

Of these characteristics, that of hope deserves special mention in this context. In the early centuries of Christain history it was the conviction that this life is not all, that there is fulfillment, even though we cannot see it now, which most set Christians apart. Christians handled the ambiguities of their present life, even death as martyrs, by looking toward an eternal crown that they would one day obtain. They did not allow themselves to be overwhelmed with despair, even in the collapse of Roman civilization, because they knew "we have no enduring city here" (Heb. 13:17) but looked always for a greater, a heavenly one (Heb. 11:16). In the Middle Ages, admittedly, they may have carried their other-worldly outlook to an extreme, and the redress of balance that came with the Renaissance was perhaps wholesome.

That the pendulum may have swung too far in the past century or so, however, is attested by the growth of nihilism and absolute skepticism. A welcome response has come in the form of the theology of hope, a product of Christian-Marxist dialogue. Marxists such as Roger Garaudy had to remind Christians not to let their most important message, that of hope, slip away. In our day, as in Paul's, it is essential that we not grieve "as others . . . who have no hope (1 Thess. 4:13). Does any characteristic testify more eloquently to our faith's credibility when we confront the exigencies of our existence? Does any characteristic offer more assistance to go on in spite of it all?

It is not necessary to speak further in this chapter of a third channel for effecting the Christian mission, *Christian action*. It will not be superfluous, however, to reiterate the importance of incarnation. It never suffices simply to say, "I love everybody." Even if our opportunities to put love in action touch mostly other believers, we do not want to set limits to love's action. We are to love even our enemies

(Matt. 5:44) if we would fulfill Christ's instruction.

A Vigilant People

Because science and technology figure so largely in the human city, it behooves us to comment more fully on the attitude of the churches toward them. As I indicated earlier, this attitude should reflect neither unqualified approval nor unfailing censure. The churches have probably erred more often in the latter than in the former and at considerable cost. It is unquestionably correct to say that negative criticism has widened the rift between the churches and the scientists, the foundation for whose method was laid by the church. One need mention here only the celebrated censure of Galileo by the Roman Church, but it by no means stood alone. As moderners have turned to the scientist for the last word about matters of life and death, it is not surprising to hear a Cambridge anthropologist boldly assert that scientists "have a right to play God." Already they do so in terms of creativity; now they must do so in terms of morality.[8]

Hopefully the chasm is not yet as unbridgeable as this quotation may imply. As a matter of fact, there are promising signs that the scientific community is casting an eye toward the churches, asking for cooperation in working toward solutions to humanity's problems. Indeed, there are signs that a new openness is appearing in scientific method, one that will speak less dogmatically from the scientific side and with greater amenability to dimensions of transcendence. In a conference I attended in 1974 on "The Healing of the Whole Person," for example, medical doctors spoke approvingly of faith as a part of the healing process.

From the side of the churches the signs of openness to the scientific community have been put forth more cautiously thus far. However, Teilhard de Chardin moved far down the road toward a detente. In *The Future of Man*[9] he argued that the continuing progress of human development depended on three things: (1) organization of research, (2) concentration of research on the subject of humanity, and (3) a joining of hands of science and religion. Teilhard was doubtless overly optimistic in his hopes, but some of the things he forecast have begun to appear. Not surprisingly, his thought has attracted the attention of scientists as well as believers.

However positive the relationship between Christianity and science may become, there is an urgent need for vigilance on the part of all concerned persons about the uses of science and technology. Already scientists themselves have sounded an alarm about certain uses. There are many serious issues before our society now.

1. *Development of nuclear weapons and even certain nonmilitary uses of nuclear energy.* The harmful effects of exposure to radiation is well known. What happens if nuclear weapons or plutonium for making them falls into the wrong hands?

2. *Experimentation with live fetuses.* Numerous cases have come to light recently. Is a fetus only an organism, or is it a person?

3. *Experimentation with human guinea pigs.* A few cases of the use of prisoners for this purpose have appeared. Medical doctors are now discussing whether to experiment with the unproven drug laetrile on cancer patients.

4. *Transplants of vital organs.* This has become common, but results are mixed. Heart transplant patients do not live long. Is this type of thing more than experimentation?

5. *Removal of life-support devices when the patient is medically dead.* The celebrated case of Karen Quinlan, who lived even after the plug was pulled, makes this issue still fuzzier.

6. *Sterilization of unwed mothers.* Forcible sterilization was practiced widely in India during Indira Gandhi's presidency. It has occurred several times in the United States. How far does the state have a right to go in usurping an individual's right to decide?

7. *Abortion.* A bitter battle has resulted from the Supreme Court decision to allow mothers to decide up to the sixth month of pregnancy whether to have an abortion.

8. *Euthanasia.* One or two cases of mercy killing have posed again the question of allowing people to die with dignity.

All of these are complex issues, requiring the best thought of all responsible citizens. The issues are not simply scientific. They are human; and, as such, they are spiritual. The churches hold a huge stake in how they are resolved. Most scientists would like the counsel of the churches as well as the legal judgment of the courts. We must be cautious here. There are those who would argue these cases from a crassly methodological point of view: Whatever advances science is good. From a Christian perspective, this is unacceptable. Our concern is the human and the personal. Persons must be placed above even scientific progress. Most scientists would surely agree.

Conclusion

Now that the churches have decided seriously to minister in the city, they face both frightening challenges and immense possibilities. They should be prepared for failure, for they will not succeed in the way they have in rural and small-town America. But they should be thankful they do not have to succeed in the sense that our contemporaries usually measure success. Their task within the vast complex society we see being built is to bring people a vision, a dream, of the city that God is building for humanity. Through their ministry as salt and light and soul, the churches can awaken an awareness of the transcendent reality that pervades the whole human community. Through the lives of the faithful can flow the love that binds up and heals the wounds of the lonely, the anguished, the distraught, the bereaved. Through the Chrisitan community, God's Spirit can work to effect a healing of the divisions of modern society—divisions of race, wealth, age, culture, and the rest. Once again, Christians can be to the world what the soul is to the body.

In *The Agony and the Ecstasy* Irving Stone tells about Michelangelo sculpting one of his most renowned statues. Along with Florence's greatest artist, Michelangelo was invited to bid for the sculpting of the Duccio column. The column was a huge, once-fine marble now gouged and, if handled wrong, likely to break in the center. Leonardo da Vinci declined even to bid; the job was beneath him. But Michelangelo had a dream, a vision. For hours he contemplated his creation. And when the Florentine Council accepted his bid, he made the chips fly as he released from the stone the form of his famous *David*.

Human life, humanity's life, is like the Duccio column. It is not flawless. It has been marred by the impairment of God-consciousness. What is needed is a vision, a vision of the city God is creating, of what he can and will bring into being. Such a vision belongs to the people of God.

12
The Church and the Future

This book has grappled with the urgent issue of defining the nature and mission of the church in a time of accelerated change in the shape of civilization. In recent years many have been ready to write the church's epitaph, convinced that it was too tied to the perspectives and the patterns of another era.

I have never shared this pessimism. Although in this book I have taken full cognizance of the hurricane impact the *pace* of change is having on the churches as well as individuals, I am not fearful of the future. The fact is, history gives us a certain confidence about the church's future—not a confidence based on its strengths but, paradoxically, on its weaknesses. History confirms, I think, Paul's judgment that our confidence lies not in *our* competence but in what God does to make us competent (2 Cor. 3:4-6) and that "we have this treasure in earthen vessels, to show that the transcendent power belongs to God and not to us" (2 Cor. 4:7). In a word, the church's survival and success depend on God and not on us, a fact which should reassure us about failure. The whole enterprise, thank God, does not rest on our shoulders.

Still, it matters what we, the church today, do. And, once again, history gives us some assurance. In nearly two millenia of its existence, Christianity has experienced and responded to numerous cultural shifts. At least three times in its march westward it has faced drastic cultural upheavals equivalent to the one we now confront. From the church's experience in these epochs we learn both that the church can change and yet it does not have to change just for the sake of changing.

Item 1. Christianity had scarcely emerged from the womb of Judaism before it had to make its first and perhaps most wrenching adjustment, from Jewish to Hellenistic culture. It was assisted in this, of course, by the experience of its parent. Long before Christianity arose, Judaism had begun to accommodate itself to the cultures of people of the Diaspora. This process reached its peak at the time of Christ as the Jewish people undertook a vigorous mission among the nations. Even inside of Palestine but especially outside of it, they accommodated their language, thought, dress, observances, and worship to the all-powerful Hellenistic model. The brilliant Jewish apologist of Alexandria, Philo, a contemporary of Jesus, epitomized the effort as he read the best Hellenistic wisdom into the Old Testament Scriptures.

So Christianity did not begin a new thing; it continued one. As it, following Paul's effort to be "all things to all men," essayed to adjust itself more radically even than Judaism to the culture of the Roman Empire, it inspired a conservative reaction in the latter. As a result, Christianity and not Judaism became within a remarkably brief time the dominant faith of the Roman Empire. It soon was quite at home in what had been a wholly alien land. This is not to say that all Christians adapted or wished to adapt in the same way. As we saw in an earlier chapter, they covered the whole spectrum in their opposition to or approval of this adaptation. However, their very debate proved useful, for it forced them to evaluate changes under the searchlight of the nature and mission of the church, much as we have tried to do in this volume.

Item 2. The next epochal turn came with the collapse of the western (Latin) part of the Roman Empire between A.D. 376 and 476. The numerous barbarian peoples who gradually took control of the West lacked both culture and political cohesiveness. Indeed, most of them admired Roman culture and sought to imitate it. As the one institution that retained some sense of unity and continuity with the past, the church stepped in to fill the cultural and political vacuum as the so-called Dark Ages opened. It does not deserve the blame often heaped on it for the decay of civilization. That was a product of the barbarian invasions. Quite to the contrary, the church gradually inspired the formation of a new, essentially Christian, culture and the civilization of the Middle Ages that we call Christendom. Again, it proved its ability to change without losing its identity, always keeping before itself one of the images of the church which we have expounded; the city of God.

Item 3. The third major shift, the Renaissance, began around 1300 and has continued to exert an influence up to this very time. The Renaissance had to do essentially with a radical alteration in human self-understanding and, consequently, in the understanding of authority. It represented a change from the church to the individual conscience as final arbiter of truth. Individual consciousness that began to appear in the fourteenth century has grown apace and is manifest in the authority crisis of the twentieth century.

Not all persons or institutions looked with equal favor upon the changes occurring in their civilization. The humanists who led the accommodation represented a cultured minority. In the sixteenth century Protestants, for the most part, were more partial to the shift than those remaining in the Roman Church. The Reformers opted for the "modern devotion" of Erasmus and the humanists. They closed monasteries. They spoke of vocation in terms of service in the world and not withdrawal from it. They adjusted their life-styles to fit the new times. Here, too, however, they measured change from the vantage point of early Christian experience much as I have proposed that we do today; they did not advocate change for its own sake.

Having reviewed Christianity's response to change in the past, however, does not solve our current problems with it. To change is frightening. It places individuals, groups, and societies under immense stress. The most effective way to cope with it, as Toffler has observed, is to formulate certain principles for planning and pacing our lives. Persons and groups having a fairly clear grasp of who they are and what their purpose is stand the best chance of handling the impact of accelerated change.

As far as the nature and purpose of the church are concerned, there is much, no doubt legitimate, debate regarding what is required. Some would argue, "Christ alone"; others would emphasize "the now visible institutional expression which can be aligned with the traditions of the past." I have argued that both of these approaches are inadequate. The first leaves too little, the second too much to identify the church and its mission.

To be sure, the church should always place Christ at the center. However, can we know Christ in our generation apart from an embodiment in the lives of believers who unfailingly experience him in terms of their culture? The first Christian generations could not. Neither can any other generation. For each generation Christ is our life in terms of our common experience—whether through gathering in worship or scattering in the world, through organizing to discharge our mission or actually implementing it. We cannot reduce Christianity to an experience or an idea. It involves living and acting out what we believe. If we don't act it out, then we don't even believe it.

Still, I am not proposing that we feel ourselves bound to carry the baggage of the centuries or even of our own day. If we cannot reduce Christianity to an "essence," neither can we define it in terms of rites and rituals, programs and organizations, bureaucracies and hierarchies. It is people. And nothing is as important for us to remember as that fact. It is the people of God on mission in and to the world.

In the end, then, I propose that we steer between these two extremes. To understand the church, we may begin with certain primal images from the Scriptures. But we cannot stop there. We also have to contemplate how these images become incarnate in human beings in particular times and cultures. We cannot rest content with thinking of the church as "a purely spiritual entity," as Rudolph Sohm, great nineteenth-century German jurist, once did. We have to think how spirit and flesh together constitute the new humanity, the people of God, the servant, the city of God. We could hardly act more in contradiction of the church's nature as defined by these images than to leave ourselves disembodied.

The effort of people to be the church means, therefore, to exercise faith, for we are always striving to reach an unattainable goal that we must strive nonetheless to attain. It is presumptuous for us to contemplate that we are not just people, worldly people, but *God's* people. It is mind blowing to think that we, sinful and finite human beings, play a role in the divine purpose for humanity. Yet that is precisely what the Scriptures say about the church. How can they make such an assertion?

They base this claim upon the conviction that God, Creator and Sovereign of the universe, has initiated it. He has chosen us; we have not chosen him. He has covenanted with us to be our God; we have responded by covenanting to be his people, with all the rights, privileges, and responsibilities that implies. He stands ready to use us as the instruments of his purpose for humanity insofar as we yield ourselves to him.

In the last analysis, here is where our confidence in the face of accelerated change rests. Like Abraham, we can set out for a land and circumstances we cannot foresee (Heb. 11:8). We can be aliens and exiles, strangers where we live, because we know that the One who made the promise to us is faithful (Heb. 11:13). We will not change just for the sake of changing or because others are doing so, but because *he* has called us to this continuing pilgrimage.

Notes

CHAPTER 1

1. Alvin Toffler, *Future Shock* (New York: Random House, 1970).
2. Ross MacKenzie, *Trying New Sandals* (Atlanta: John Knox Press, 1973), pp. 103 ff.

CHAPTER 2

1. *Profession of the Tridentine Faith*, article X in *The Creeds of Christendom* 2 (New York: Harper and Brothers, 1877): 209.
2. *The Papal Syllabus of Errors*, article 18; in ibid., pp. 217-218.
3. *First Dogmatic Constitution on the Church of Christ*, chapter 3; in ibid., p. 263.
4. Hans Küng, *Infallible? An Inquiry.*, trans. Edward Quinn (Garden City, New York: Doubleday and Co., 1970). For a fuller review of the entire controversy see *The Infallibility Debate*, ed. John J. Kirvan (Paramus, N.J.: Paulist Press, 1971).
5. Harold Lindsell, *The Battle for the Bible* (Grand Rapids, Michigan: Zondervan Publishing House, 1976), p. 18.
6. Ibid., p. 25.

CHAPTER 3

1. Oscar Cullmann, *Christ and Time*, trans. Floyd V. Filson (Philadelphia: Westminster Press, 1950).
2. *Epistle to Diognetus*, 5.8-9, 17.
3. Ibid., 6.1.
4. The Shepherd of Hermas, *Similitudes*, 1.6.
5. *Against Celsus*, 8.74-75.
6. In Eusebius of Caesarea, *Life of Constantine*, 4.24.
7. Eusebius, *Praises of Constantine*, 8.

CHAPTER 4

1. The Bull *Unam Sanctam* (1302), in *Documents of the Christian Church*, ed. Henry Bettenson (New York and London: Oxford University Press, 1947), p. 163.

2. Alfred Loisy, *The Gospel and The Church*, trans. Christopher Home (New York: Charles Scribner's Sons, 1912), p. 166.

3. Oscar Cullmann, *Peter: Disciple—Apostle—Martyr*, trans. Floyd V. Filson (London: SCM Press Ltd., 1953), pp. 180 ff.

4. Albert Schweitzer, *The Quest of the Historical Jesus* (London: Adam and Charles Black, 1954), pp. 368-369.

5. C. H. Dodd, *The Parables of the Kingdom* (New York: Charles Scribner's Sons Ltd., 1935), p. 48.

6. Ibid., pp. 79-80.

7. Werner Georg Kummel, *Promise and Fulfillment*, trans. Dorothea M. Barton (Naperville, Illinois: Alec R. Allenson, Inc., 1957), p. 47.

8. Eduard Schweizer, "Studies in Biblical Theology," no. 28, *Lordship and Discipleship* (London: SCM Press Ltd., 1960), p. 20.

9. T. W. Manson, *The Teaching of Jesus: Studies in Its Form and Content* (Cambridge: University Press, 1955), pp. 3-21.

10. John Wick Bowman, *The Intention of Jesus* (Philadelphia: Westminster Press, 1943), pp. 213-214.

11. A. M. Hunter, *A Pattern for Life: an Exposition of the Sermon on the Mount* (Philadelphia: Westminster Press, 1953), p. 113.

12. Bowman, p. 221.

13. Oscar Cullmann, "The Kingship of Christ and the Church in the New Testament," *The Early Church*, ed. A. J. B. Higgins (London; SCM Press Ltd., 1966), p. 119.

14. Ibid., p. 123.

15. W. F. Albright and C. S. Mann, "Matthew," *The Anchor Bible* (Garden City, New York: Doubleday and Co., 1971), p. 197.

CHAPTER 5

1. H. Richard Niebuhr, *Christ and Culture* (New York: Harper and Brothers, 1951), p. 49.

2. *On the Spectacles*, 24.4

3. *Hutterite Chronicle* (New York: Cayuga Press, 1943), p. 47.

4. Quoted by Epiphanius, *Panarion*, 33.3-7.

5. *Life of Constantine*, 3.1; NPNF, 1, 519-20.

6. *The Secular City* (New York: Macmillan Co., 1965), p. 65.

7. *Conf.* 13.27.43.

CHAPTER 6

1. *Schism in the Early Church* (London: SCM Press, Ltd., 1964), pp. 212-215.
2. *Trying New Sandals* (Atlanta: John Knox Press, 1973), pp. 103-106.

CHAPTER 7

1. *Traditional Symbols and the Contemporary World* (London: Epworth Press, 1973).
2. Gaines S. Dobbins, *Building Better Churches* (Nashville: Broadman Press, 1947), pp. 178-180.

CHAPTER 8

1. C. H. Dodd, *The Apostolic Preaching and Its Developments* (London: Hodder and Stonghton, Ltd., 1936).
2. *Pesahim* 10.5; *The Mishnah*, trans. Herbert Danby (London: Oxford, 1933), p. 151; italics mine.

CHAPTER 9

1. *Res gestae*, 22.5.4; LCL 2, 202.

CHAPTER 10

1. *Epistle* 22, To Arsacius; Loeb Classical Library 2, 71.
2. Thomas C. Campbell and Yoshio Fukuyama, *The Fragmented Layman: an Empirical Study of Lay Attitudes* (Philadelphia: Pilgrim Press, 1970).
3. This material is a condensation of the author's article on "A Rationale for Baptist Higher Education," *Search*, Fall 1973, pp. 11-21.

CHAPTER 11

1. *The Church Inside Out*, trans. Isaac C. Rottenberg (Philadelphia: The Westminster Press, 1966), p. 113.
2. Fuller statistics may be found in Arnold Toynbee, *The Industrial Revolution* (Boston: Beacon Press, 1956), p. 10.
3. In *A History of Christianity,* ed. Clyde L. Manschreck (Englewood Cliffs, New Jersey: Prentice-Hall, Inc., 1964), p. 383.
4. Ibid., p. 385.

5. The accounts of creation in Genesis 1 and 2:4 to 3:24 make a slightly different point here. The latter makes quite clear that humanity was made to acknowledge God's dominion, to be submissive. Its positing of the fall in eating from the fruit of the tree of knowledge of good and evil would not imply necessarily a negative attitude toward science as much as a condemnation of the human tendency to usurp the Creator's place and to deny creatureliness.

6. Alfred Delp, *The Prison Meditations of Father Delp* (New York: The Macmillan Co., 1963), p. 93.

7. Thomas Merton, *Faith and Violence* (South Bend, Indiana: University of Notre Dame, 1968), pp. 216-17.

8. Edmund R. Leach, "We Scientists Have the Right to Play God," *Look*, December 1968, pp. 16, 20.

9. Pierre Teilhard de Chardin, *The Future of Man*, trans. Norman Denny (New York: Harper and Row, 1964), pp. 227-231.